FOR SUPERFINE COOKERY.

HOWARDS' SODA

is absolutely pure and practically

TASTELESS

Used in the

BEST KITCHENS

for over

100 YEARS

HOWARDS & SONS, Ltd

Est. 1797.

Ilford, nr. LONDON.

Makers of HOWARDS' ASPIRIN TABLETS.

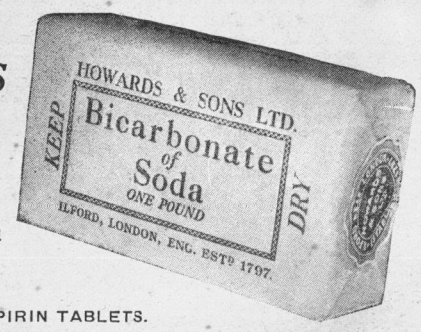

The Famous Sister Products

FREE FROM PRESERVATIVES

COOK'S SUET

Best Beef Suet in fine shreds—the most convenient and economical form. Far superior to raw suet and makes infinitely better cooking. In $\frac{1}{4}$, $\frac{1}{2}$ and 1 lb. cartons from all grocers.

COOK'S FARM EGGS

"Pure New-Laid Eggs in Golden Flakes." Perfect for every culinary purpose. Never disappoint. Far more economical than ordinary shell eggs. Ask your grocer for them.

FREE SAMPLES ON APPLICATION.

DONALD COOK & SON, LTD., 19/20, WEST SMITHFIELD, LONDON, E.C.1

Whenever the book says cream —

"A quarter pint of cream" says the cookery book. But look at the price of cream! A shillingsworth goes nowhere. What's a girl to do? Why, use "Ideal" Milk instead. For thick creamy Soups and Sauces, for delicious Savouries and Sweets, whenever Mrs. Beeton says cream you can say "Ideal" Milk.

"Ideal" Milk is the best of the country milk concentrated. It is just like cream in everything except that it costs so much less and goes so much further.

"IDEAL" MILK
Unsweetened

PREPARED BY NESTLÉ'S IN ENGLAND

HORS D'ŒUVRE DISHES AND SAVOURIES

1. Cheese Soufflés. 2. Angels on Horseback. 3. Prawns à la Tartare.
4. Anchovy Croûtes. 5. Celery à la Rivaz. 6. Mayonnaise of Eggs.
7. Fancy Butter. 8. Assorted Hors d'Œuvre.

MRS. BEETON'S
HORS d'ŒUVRE
AND SAVOURIES

INCLUDING CHEESE AND EGG DISHES, SANDWICHES, SALADS AND DRESSINGS

350 RECIPES

FULLY ILLUSTRATED

WARD, LOCK & CO., LIMITED
LONDON AND MELBOURNE

UNIFORM VOLUMES.

MRS. BEETON'S

JAM-MAKING
INCLUDING
PRESERVES, MARMALADES, PICKLES AND HOME-MADE WINES

CAKE-MAKING
INCLUDING
BUNS, BISCUITS AND OTHER DAINTIES

PUDDINGS AND PIES
INCLUDING
TARTS, SOUFFLES, OMELETS AND FRITTERS

COLD SWEETS
INCLUDING
JELLIES, CREAMS, FRUIT DISHES, COLD PUDDINGS AND ICES

SAUCES AND SOUPS
INCLUDING
SAUCES FOR FISH, MEAT, VEGETABLES AND PUDDINGS, ALSO BROTHS, AND THICK AND CLEAR SOUPS

HORS D'ŒUVRE AND SAVOURIES
INCLUDING
CHEESE AND EGG DISHES, SANDWICHES, SALADS AND DRESSINGS

POULTRY AND GAME
INCLUDING
SUITABLE SAUCES, FORCEMEATS, TRUSSING AND CARVING
300 RECIPES

FISH COOKERY
INCLUDING
SUITABLE SAUCES, SERVING AND CARVING
350 RECIPES

Printed in Great Britain by C. Tinling & Co., Ltd.,
Liverpool, London, and Prescot.

CONTENTS

CHAP.		PAGE
I	Hors d'Œuvres	5
II	Savouries	29
III	Cheese Savouries	71
IV	Egg Dishes	79
V	Sandwiches	93
VI	Salads	105
VII	Sauces and Salad Dressings	121
	Index	125

ILLUSTRATIONS

FACING PAGE

HORS D'ŒUVRE DISHES AND SAVOURIES:
    Cheese Soufflés—Angels on Horseback—Prawns à la Tartare—Anchovy Croûtes—Celery à la Rivaz—Mayonnaise of Eggs—Fancy Butter—Assorted Hors d'Œuvres . . . . . *Frontispiece*

SAVOURIES:
    Anchovy Fingers — Caviare Croustades — Sardines Devilled 16

CHEESE AND EGG DISHES:
    Cheese d'Artois—Scrambled Eggs—Cold Cheese Creams   32

CHEESE AND EGG DISHES:
    Cheese Straws—Scotch Eggs—Cheese Tartlets . . 49

DRESSED VEGETABLES:
    Wafer Potatoes—Mushroom Soufflés—Stuffed Tomatoes   64

EGG DISHES:
    Eggs Colbert Style—Eggs in Aspic—Eggs and Rice . 81

SANDWICHES:
    Chicken and Ham Sandwiches—Cheese Sandwiches—Cucumber Sandwiches 96

EGG DISHES:
    Eggs à la Courtet—Eggs à la Dreux—Anchovy Eggs . 113

CHAPTER I

HORS D'ŒUVRES

The hors d'œuvres course forms a so-called prelude to a complete dinner and consists of a variety of little dishes, both plain and dressed. These dishes, to the thoughtful cook, present one of the best opportunities for showing her skill and originality in combination and garnish.

Whatever the hors d'œuvres may consist of, let it be remembered that these little side dishes are intended to stimulate, and not to satisfy the appetite, i.e., they must be tempting and smart in appearance, and the portions must be very small, so as not to impair the enjoyment of the remainder of the meal.

These dishes are frequently placed on the table before the guests enter the dining-room, and when dressed in a pretty and dainty manner add greatly to the effective decoration of a table.

SIMPLE HORS D'ŒUVRE DISHES

Under this heading numerous articles may be used, the most popular being oysters, caviare, sardines, olives (plain and stuffed), thickly-sliced salmi, smoked ham, Bologna and other smoked sausages, and a variety of comestibles of this kind, such as, pickled tunny, anchovies, smoked eel, salmon, smoked breast of goose, foie-gras, pâté, etc., which are all usually carefully trimmed and dished up in oblong boat-shaped dishes. The manner of serving these is a matter of taste. It is, however, essential that all dishes served as hors d'œuvres should be daintily dressed. Small salad, hard-boiled yolk and white of egg, parsley, aspic jelly, etc., frequently serve as garnishing for these dishes.

BUTTER AS HORS D'ŒUVRES

A number of simple hors d'œuvres may be prepared with various kinds of compound butters, such as Montpelier, anchovy, lobster, crayfish, shrimp ravigote, maître d'hôtel, or horseradish butter, full instructions for preparing these will be found in a later chapter. Any of the above-named can be shaped into little balls, tiny pats, or cubes, and served on little squares of crisp toast, very small lunch biscuits, or thin Parmesan cheese biscuits.

Little balls of fresh butter are sometimes dished neatly on small china or glass hors d'œuvre dishes. In that case, little pieces of crisp toast or thin dry biscuits should be handed round at the same time.

RECIPES FOR HORS D'ŒUVRES

ANCHOVIES, FRIED. (Anchois frits.)

Procure 12 anchovies and for the batter take 3 oz. of flour, $\frac{1}{4}$ of a pint of tepid water, 1 tablespoonful of salad-oil, or clarified butter and the white of 1 egg.

Wipe the anchovies with a dry cloth. Sieve the flour, and mix it into a smooth batter with the water and salad oil. Whisk the white of egg stiffly, and stir it lightly into the batter. Have ready a deep pan of hot frying-fat; dip the anchovies carefully into the batter, drop them into the hot fat, and fry until they acquire a golden-brown colour. This dish is also suitable for a savoury.

This should be sufficient for 8 or 9 persons.

Note.—Anchovies are obtainable all the year round.

ANCHOVIES, RUTLAND STYLE. (Anchois à la Rutland.)

For the cheese paste have ready 3 oz. of flour, $1\frac{1}{2}$ oz. of butter, 1 dessertspoonful of grated Parmesan cheese, the yolk of 1 egg, water and a little salt and cayenne. For the anchovy preparation : 4 anchovies, 1 hard-boiled egg, 1 tablespoonful of thick white sauce, cayenne, a few drops of anchovy-essence and carmine or cochineal, and a few leaves of watercress or chervil.

Rub the butter into the flour, add the cheese, yolk of egg, a little salt and cayenne, and water to mix to a stiff paste. Roll out thinly, cut into $1\frac{3}{4}$-inch squares, bake them in a moderate oven until crisp, and use when cool. Wash, bone and dry the anchovies, and divide them into fine $\frac{1}{2}$-inch strips. Mix with them the white sauce and the finely-sieved yolk of egg, season with cayenne, add a few drops of anchovy-essence and carmine, drop by drop, until a pale pink colour is obtained. Pile the preparation on the cheese biscuits, garnish with fine strips of white of egg, and leaves of watercress or chervil.

This should be sufficient for 6 or 8 persons.

ANCHOVY BISCUITS, ROYAL. (Biscuits d'Anchois à la Royale.)

For the paste take 3 oz. of flour, 1½ oz. of butter, ½ an egg, ½ a teaspoonful of essence of anchovy and a little water. For the anchovy cream : 4 anchovies, 1 hard-boiled yolk of egg, 1 dessertspoonful of clarified butter, 3 tablespoonfuls of cream, a few grains of cayenne, a few drops of carmine or cochineal and a sprig or two of watercress.

Rub the butter into the flour, add the egg, anchovy-essence, and water to mix to a stiff paste. Roll out thinly, stamp into rounds 1¾ inches in diameter, bake in a moderate oven until crisp, and use when cool. Wash, bone and dry the anchovies, pound them with the yolk of egg and clarified butter until smooth, season with a little cayenne, and rub through a fine sieve. Whip the cream stiffly, stir the fish preparation in lightly, and add the colouring drop by drop until a pale pink is obtained. By means of a forcing-bag fill the centre of each biscuit in the form of a cone. Decorate tastefully with leaves of watercress, and serve.

This should be sufficient for 6 or 8 persons.

ANCHOVY D'ARTOIS. (D'Artois aux Anchois.)

With 1 tablespoonful of anchovy paste take 1½ tablespoonfuls of grated Parmesan cheese, 1 tablespoonful of cream or white sauce, a few grains of cayenne, 1 egg, 5 or 6 oz. of puff-paste, olives and a little anchovy butter.

Moisten the anchovy paste with sufficient cream or white sauce to enable it to be easily spread. Roll the puff-paste out three times, sprinkling it each time with cheese and a very little cayenne pepper. Finally roll it into a strip 6 inches wide and about a ¼ of an inch in thickness, and cut it in half lengthwise. Spread the anchovy preparation on one half, and cover this with the other, then cut it into strips 1 inch wide, and trim them to a uniform size. Bake in a quick oven until the paste has risen and set, then brush over with egg and sprinkle with cheese. Bake again until brown and let cool; garnish with olives halved and filled with anchovy butter.

This should be sufficient for 6 or 7 persons.

ANCHOVY EGGS. (Anchois aux Œufs.)

Have ready 4 anchovies, 4 hard-boiled eggs, 2 tablespoonfuls of white sauce, 1 teaspoonful of essence of anchovy, a few sprigs of watercress, oil and vinegar, and a few grains of cayenne.

Cut the eggs across in halves, remove the yolks carefully, and cut off the extreme end of each half to enable them to stand firmly. Wash, bone and dry the anchovies, chop them coarsely, and pound them with the yolks of eggs till smooth. Add the anchovy-essence, and the white sauce gradually until a moist paste is formed; then season to taste, and rub through a hair sieve. Fill the white of egg cases with the preparation, garnish with watercress seasoned with oil and vinegar, and serve.

This should be sufficient for 8 persons.

ANCHOVY ROLLS. (Paupiettes d'Anchois.)

Procure 2 small thin cucumbers, some oil and vinegar, anchovy fillets, crab or lobster meat, mayonnaise sauce, and pimiento.

Peel the cucumbers and cut them into inch-thick slices. Stamp out the centre portion of each by means of a column cutter. Place them on a dish, and pour over enough oil and vinegar to soak and cover. Pound the crab or lobster meat, and season with a little mayonnaise. Drain the cucumber shapes and fill the cavity with this mixture. Twist a whole anchovy fillet round each, and place a small round of pimiento on top. Dish up, garnish with parsley, and serve.

Allow 1 roll for each person and one over.

ANCHOVY TARTLETS. (Tartlettes d'Anchois.)

Prepare some anchovy paste and anchovy cream (*see* **Anchovy Biscuits**, p. 7) and have at hand some capers, lobster coral or Krona pepper.

Line very small patty-pans with the paste, prick it all over, cover the paste with buttered paper, and fill with rice. Bake in a moderately hot oven until crisp, remove the paper and rice, and when cold fill with the anchovy cream. The mixture should be piled high in the centre, and sprinkled with lobster coral or Krona pepper, the base of each being garnished with capers.

This should be sufficient for 6 or 8 persons.

ASPARAGUS SALAD WITH SHRIMPS. (Salade d'Asperges aux Crevettes.)

Procure $\frac{1}{2}$ a bundle of green asparagus and $\frac{1}{2}$ a pint of shrimps, and have ready some mayonnaise sauce and hard-boiled egg.

Prepare and cook the asparagus. When cold cut the tender portions into small pieces and put them into a bowl with the shrimps picked. Mix lightly with enough mayonnaise sauce to dress. Serve on a dish in the centre of a border of sliced hard-boiled egg.

This should be sufficient for 4 or 5 persons.

BÂTEAUX À L'EPICURIENNE.

For the pastry take $\frac{1}{4}$ of a lb. of flour, $\frac{1}{2}$ an egg, 1 tablespoonful of grated cheese and a pinch of cayenne. For the mixture: 4 oz. of Astrachan caviare, 1 tablespoonful of lemon-juice, 1 hard-boiled yolk of egg, a good pinch of paprika pepper. Savoury butter or cream for garnish. Rice paper.

Make the nouille pastry, roll out thinly, and line 8 small boat-shaped moulds with it. Prick with a fork to prevent blistering whilst being baked, and fill with rice; make 8 thin strips for masts. Bake to a golden-brown colour, remove the rice from the cases and let them cool. Rub the hard-boiled yolk of egg through a sieve, add the caviare, paprika pepper, and lemon-juice. Mix well with a wooden skewer.

Fill the little boat crusts with the caviare mixture. Ornament the edges with savoury butter or cream, insert in the centre of each a mast and sail made of a triangular-shaped piece of rice-paper fixed to one of the thin strips of baked nouille pastry. Heat up in a sharp oven for about 3 minutes, then dish up and serve. This dish is equally nice served cold; in that case force out little dots of whipped cream, slightly seasoned with paprika pepper, round the edge of each little boat.

This should be sufficient for 8 persons.

BEETROOT CASSOLETTES. (Cassolettes de Betterave.)

Have ready some cooked beetroot and vinegar marinade. For the salpicon take some anchovy fillets, hard-boiled white of egg, gherkins, salt, pepper, oil, vinegar, chopped parsley, and other herbs.

Cut 8 or more cassolette shapes from the cooked beetroot, and steep them in the vinegar marinade. Prepare the salpicon by cutting the ingredients into slices or julienne strips. Season with salt, pepper, oil and vinegar, and mix with the parsley and other herbs. Drain the cassolettes and fill them with the salpicon. Dish up, garnish, and serve very cold.

Allow 1 cassolette for each person.

BEETROOT, DRESSED. (Betterave à l'Orientale.)

To 1 small cooked beetroot allow 2 anchovies, 2 hard-boiled eggs, 1 tablespoonful of finely-chopped capers, 1 very finely-chopped shallot, anchovy-essence, lemon-juice, thin slices of brown bread, butter, and a good seasoning of pepper, cayenne and salt.

Prepare some thin slices of brown bread and butter, cut from them 8 or 9 rounds about $1\frac{3}{4}$ inches in diameter, and cover them with slices of beetroot of corresponding size and thickness. Cut the eggs across into thin slices, select 8 or 9 of suitable size, remove the yolk, and place the rings of white of egg on the bread and butter croûtes, leaving visible a narrow margin of beetroot. Pass the remainder of the eggs through a sieve, mix with them the capers and shallot, add a few drops of lemon-juice and sufficient anchovy-essence to form a moist paste. Season to taste, pile the preparation in the centre of the croûtes, garnish with fine strips of anchovies, and serve.

This should be sufficient for 6 or 7 persons.

CANAPÉS.

Canapés are made of either toasted or fried bread, cut into suitably shaped slices. In most cases canapés or croûtes are best if fried in butter to a golden colour. They must be well drained and cooled before being used. Plain water biscuits, or wafer biscuits, are also used at times as the basis for canapés. Canapés described in this chapter can be served either at the beginning of a meal or at the end.

CAVIARE AND PRAWNS. (Caviar aux Crevettes.)

Have ready 1½ oz. of caviare, 32 small prawns, capers, 1 lemon, ½ a shallot very finely chopped, thin slices of brown bread, butter and cayenne.

Prepare thin slices of brown bread and butter, cut from them 8 or 9 rounds about 1½ inches in diameter, and cover them with thin slices of lemon trimmed to the size of the croûte. Add the shallot and a few drops of lemon-juice to the caviare, season with cayenne, and stir with a wooden spoon or skewer. Pile the preparation on the croûtes; with the point of a wooden skewer hollow the centre down to the lemon, and fill the cavity with capers. Arrange 4 picked prawns in a nearly upright equi-distant position, then send to table.

This should be sufficient for 6 or 7 persons.

Note.—Caviare is in season all the year round, fresh caviare is at its best during the spring.

CAVIARE CROUSTADES. (Croustades au Caviar.)

Procure 1 small pot of caviare and have at hand 1 dessertspoonful of lemon-juice, 1 finely-chopped shallot, slices of stale bread about ½ to ¾ of an inch in thickness, clarified butter and some anchovy butter (p. 102).

From the slices of stale bread cut or stamp out 9 or more rounds, ovals, or squares 2 inches in diameter, and with a smaller cutter, or a knife, make an inner circle, oval, or square ⅓ of an inch from the outer edge of the croustade. Fry them carefully in clarified butter until lightly browned, then with the point of a small sharp knife lift out the inner ring, remove all moist crumbs, place them in a moderate oven to become crisp and dry, and cool before using. Add the shallot and lemon-juice to as much caviare as will be required to fill the cases, stir well with a wooden skewer, and put the preparation into the cases. Make the anchovy butter as directed, put it into a forcing-bag or paper cornet, and decorate the border of each croustade. Serve cold.

This should be sufficient for 8 or 9 persons.

CELERY À LA GRECQUE.

Have ready the heart portion of 2 heads of white celery, some vinaigrette sauce (p. 124) and 1 dessertspoonful finely-chopped fennel leaves.

Clean the celery and shred finely. Put into a pie-dish and pour over a well-made "Vinaigrette." Sprinkle the chopped fennel leaves over, cover, and allow to stand for about 2 hours, range tastefully on a hors d'œuvre dish, and serve.

This should be sufficient for 4 or more persons.

CELERY À LA RIVAZ.

Take the white part of 2 heads of celery and 1 good-sized pickled beetroot and prepare some tartare sauce (p. 124).

Wash, trim, and cook the celery till tender, cut into fine strips or shreds. Peel the beetroot and cut it into strips. Mix both together with enough tartare sauce to season the salad well, then range on a hors d'œuvre dish, and serve.

This should be sufficient for 7 or more persons.

CHEESE BISCUITS WITH CREAM. (Biscuits de Fromage à la Crème.)

Take 4 oz. of best flour, 4 oz. of grated Parmesan cheese, 3 oz. of butter, 2 yolks of eggs, $\frac{1}{2}$ a gill of cream, $\frac{1}{2}$ a lemon, a saltspoonful of salt, a little cayenne and Krona pepper.

Rub the butter into the flour, add 3 oz. of cheese, a saltspoonful of salt and a good pinch of cayenne, and mix into a VERY stiff paste with the yolk of eggs and lemon-juice, adding a few drops of milk if necessary. Roll out to about $\frac{1}{8}$ of an inch in thickness, stamp out some rounds $1\frac{3}{4}$ inches in diameter, prick them with a fork, and bake them in a moderately cool oven until crisp, then let them get cool. Whip the cream stiffly, stir in the remainder of the cheese, add a pinch of cayenne; force out, by means of a forcing-bag or paper cornet, a little pyramid in the centre of each biscuit. Sprinkle with Krona pepper, and serve cold on a folded napkin or dish-paper. These, although frequently served as hors d'œuvres, are perhaps more suitable when served as savouries.

This should be sufficient for 7 or 8 persons.

CHEESE CREAM, COLD. (Crème au Fromage froid.)

Have ready $\frac{3}{4}$ of an oz. of grated Parmesan cheese, $\frac{3}{4}$ of an oz. of grated Gruyère or Cheddar cheese, 1 gill of cream, $\frac{1}{2}$ a gill of aspic jelly, made mustard, cayenne, Krona pepper, salt and a few sprigs of watercress.

Season the cheese with a mustardspoonful of made mustard,

a saltspoonful of salt, and a good pinch of cayenne, then add to these ingredients the aspic jelly, previously stiffly whipped. Whip the cream until stiff, stir it in lightly, turn the preparation into paper soufflé cases, put them aside in a cool place for 1 hour, then sprinkle with Krona pepper, garnish with watercress, and serve. Or, the mixture may be put into small dariole moulds, previously coated with aspic jelly, and decorated with chilli, etc. These, although frequently served as hors d'œuvres, are perhaps most suitable as savouries.

This should be sufficient for 6 or 7 persons.

CHEESE CREAM CROÛTES. (Croûtes de Fromage.)

Prepare some cheese mixture with the same ingredients as in the preceding recipe, and have ready some croûtes of fried bread 1¾ inches in diameter, chopped aspic jelly, watercress, Krona pepper, salad oil and vinegar.

Spread the cheese cream mixture on the bottom of a sauté-pan or shallow baking-tin, and when set cut it into rounds the same size as the croûtes. Sprinkle each round with a little Krona pepper, and serve garnished with chopped aspic jelly and watercress seasoned with salad-oil and vinegar. These may also be served as savoury.

This should be sufficient for 6 or 7 persons.

CHEESE ZÉPHIRES. (Zéphires au Parmesan.)

Take 3 heaped tablespoonfuls of Parmesan cheese, 1 oz. of gelatine, ½ a pint of cream, ½ a pint of milk, cayenne, salt, chopped aspic jelly and shredded truffle and pimiento.

Soak the gelatine in the milk for ½ an hour, then stir it over the fire until it is dissolved. Let it cool, add the cheese, the cream previously stiffly whipped, and seasoning to taste. Turn into oval fluted zéphire moulds, set on ice or in a very cool place until firm, then unmould, and serve garnished with chopped aspic jelly and shredded truffle and pimiento.

This should be sufficient for 6 or 7 persons.

Note.—By changing the shape of the mould, the term Zéphire may be applied to many of the preparations described as Darioles, Timbales and Soufflés.

CRAYFISH. (Écrevisses.)

Crayfish, which must not be confounded with crawfish, are similar to lobsters, only much smaller. The flesh is most delicate. They are extremely useful for side dishes, as well as for garnishing cold and hot entrées. There are several kinds, the best being those which are quite red under the claws. Prawns are often used in their place when crayfish cannot be obtained. They are boiled in water, with plenty of salt in it, for about 10 minutes.

To serve them in shells, cut the ends of lemons so as to make them stand, stick the horns of crayfish or prawns into the lemons in circular rows, commencing at the bottom of a lemon. Fill up the vacant spaces with freshly-picked parsley, and arrange them neatly upon the dish in which they are served. This is called a pyramid of prawns or crayfish as the case may be.

CUCUMBER. (Concombre.)

Have ready 1 large cucumber, salad-oil, French wine vinegar, chopped parsley and salt.

Peel the cucumber thinly and cut into thin slices. Lay the slices on a dish, and sprinkle with salt, cover, and let them remain thus for 1 or 2 hours. Drain well, dish up on small glass dishes, season with a little salad-oil and French wine vinegar. Sprinkle over the top a little finely-chopped parsley, and serve.

This should be sufficient for 10 or 12 persons.

CUCUMBER BARQUETTES. (Barquettes de Concombre.)

Procure 1 or 2 large cucumbers, salad-oil and vinegar, smoked salmon, a few capers and gherkins and a little salad dressing.

Cut the cucumber into boat-shapes, and scoop out the centre part of each. Steep for about 1 hour in a marinade of oil and vinegar. Mix together the smoked salmon, capers, and gherkins, and season with salad dressing. Fill the little boats with the mixture, dish up, garnish tastefully and serve.

Allow 1 little boat-shape for each person.

CUCUMBER SALAD À L'ESPAGNOLE.

With 1 large or 2 small cucumbers take 1 or 2 Spanish pimientos, salad-oil, vinegar, a little finely-chopped chervil, salt and pepper.

Peel the cucumber thinly, cut in halves lengthwise and remove the seedy portion. Cut the cucumber thus prepared into very fine slices or small cube shapes. Cut the pimientos into fine strips and mix with the cubes of cucumber. Season with salt and pepper, and add enough salad-oil and vinegar to season, also the finely-chopped chervil. Mix carefully, and dish up.

This should be sufficient for 10 or 12 persons.

CUCUMBER, STUFFED, À LA JOSÉPHINE.

To 1 good-sized cucumber allow 3 oz. of cooked chicken, veal, or rabbit meat, 6 small mushrooms, 1 oz. of cooked ham, $\frac{1}{2}$ a gill of white sauce, $\frac{1}{2}$ a gill of aspic, $\frac{1}{2}$ a gill of fresh cream, brown bread, butter, lobster butter, parsley, pepper, salt and a pinch of nutmeg.

Cut the cucumber into 1-inch thick slices, peel thinly, and stamp out the inside by means of a pastry-cutter. Blanch the pieces in salted water and drain on a cloth. Pound the meat, mushrooms and ham together in a mortar, then rub through a fine sieve. Put the purée in a stewpan, season with pepper, a little salt, and a pinch of grated nutmeg. Warm up the sauce and aspic together, stir over the ice till it begins to set, then add the cream previously whipped. Stamp out some rounds of brown bread a little larger than the cucumber shapes, spread over some of the above prepared purée, then place a round of cucumber on each and fill up the centre of each with the purée (pile up high). Decorate tastefully with some creamed butter, and lobster butter. Dish up, garnish tastefully with sprigs of fresh parsley, and serve.

Allow 1 croûte for each person.

EGG MAYONNAISE.

Boil 5 fresh eggs till hard, shell them and cut each in half lengthwise ; remove the yolks and mix with a little mayonnaise sauce. Season and refill the halves of eggs. Place them on a wire tray and coat them with mayonnaise sauce, previously mixed with a little aspic jelly. When the eggs are well coated and set range them on a bed of seasoned salad (shredded lettuce or endive) on a dish. Decorate the top of each with tarragon leaves, thinly cut strips of chilli or pimiento and gherkin and serve.

EGG RÉMOULADE.

Have ready 4 or 5 hard-boiled eggs, some Rémoulade sauce (p. 122) and a few sprigs of parsley.

Cut the hard-boiled eggs in halves, take out the yolks and chop up finely, and cut the whites into fine shreds or strips. Mix the yolks with sufficient Rémoulade sauce to form a liquid seasoning. Blend with the shredded white of egg and dish up. Garnish with sprigs of parsley, and serve.

This should be sufficient for 5 or 6 persons.

EGG SALAD. (Salade aux Œufs.)

Take 5 hard-boiled eggs, oil, vinegar, salt, pepper and a few sprigs of parsley.

Shred finely or cut into small julienne strips the whites of the hard-boiled eggs. Rub the yolks through a coarse sieve, and mix with oil, vinegar, salt and pepper, then add the shredded white of egg, and blend carefully. Dish up, sprinkle over a little finely-chopped parsley, and send to table.

This should be sufficient for 6 or 7 persons.

EGGS À LA DIJON.

Have ready 2 hard-boiled eggs (whites only). For the mixture: cooked ham, foie-gras, truffle, mushrooms and seasoning.

Cut the eggs in halves, remove the yolk, and cut small thin slices off the bottom to make them stand properly. Make a purée of the ham, and mix with the foie-gras, add the truffle and mushrooms chopped, and season. Fill the white of egg with the mixture. Garnish suitably, and serve.

This should be sufficient for 4 persons.

EGGS À LA OLIVIA.

With 4 hard-boiled eggs, take a few rounds of toasted bread or plain biscuits, some cooked ham, Spanish olives, pimiento and mayonnaise sauce (p. 122).

Cut the eggs into ½-inch thick slices, remove the yolk, and place the whites on the rounds of toast or biscuits. Make a purée of the ham, and add the olives chopped. Season with mayonnaise sauce. Fill the cavities with this mixture. Place a ring of olives on top of each, with a dot of pimiento.

Allow 1 croûte for each person.

SAVOURIES

1. Anchovy Fingers. 2. Caviare Croustades. 3. Sardines Devilled.

EGGS, STUFFED, À LA RUSSE. (Œufs farcis à la Russe.)

With 6 hard-boiled eggs take some caviare, mayonnaise sauce (p. 122), a few even-sized tomatoes, parsley, oil, vinegar, salt and pepper.

Remove the shells from the eggs and cut them crosswise. Scoop out the yolks, fill in the vacant spaces with caviare, and cover with a little mayonnaise sauce with which the yolks of eggs have been incorporated. Cut the tomatoes into slices, and season with chopped parsley, oil, vinegar, salt and pepper. Serve the eggs on slices of tomatoes. Dish up, and garnish with parsley.

This should be sufficient for 10 to 12 persons.

FOIE-GRAS AS HORS D'ŒUVRE.

Foie-gras or goose liver, either in the form of pâté or sausage, is frequently served as hors d'œuvre. A pâté or terrine may be served plain after removing the fat on its surface, or scooped out by means of a dessertspoon previously dipped in hot water, and then dressed neatly on a dish, and garnished with parsley. Foie-gras sausage must be cut into thin slices, dished up and similarly garnished. In all cases, foie-gras must be served very cold, and should be kept on ice, if possible, until required.

FOIE-GRAS CROÛTES. (Croûtes de Foie-Gras.)

Have ready some foie-gras, salt and pepper, croûtes of fried or toasted bread and cream, or brown sauce.

Pound the foie-gras, adding a little cream or sauce until the right consistency is obtained. Pass through a fine sieve, season to taste, and arrange lightly on the croûtes, using a bag and forcer if available. Garnish tastefully with cream previously whipped and highly seasoned, or fancifully-cut truffle, hard-boiled white of egg, or any other suitable decoration preferred.

Allow 1 croûte to each person and 1 or 2 over.

FOIE-GRAS DARIOLES.

Put a little aspic jelly in some small plain dariole moulds, so that it sets round the sides and bottom; fill up with potted foie-gras cut into convenient slices, place on the ice for an hour, and turn out on glass dishes. Ornament with chopped cooked beetroot, hard-boiled white of egg, and thin slices of cucumber.

FOIE-GRAS, FLEURETTES.

With 1 medium-sized tin or terrine of foie-gras pâté, take 1 large truffle, 1½ gills of mayonnaise sauce (p. 122), ½ a gill of Béchamel sauce (p. 121), about ½ a pint of stiff aspic jelly, a few sprigs of tarragon and chervil, and about ¼ of an ounce of gelatine.

Have ready 6 to 8 small flat diamond-shaped entrée moulds and mask each with a thin layer of aspic jelly, then decorate them with strips of truffle and tarragon leaves. Trim the foie-gras free from fat, cut it into slices, and shape as many square slices as there are moulds, similar in shape but somewhat smaller. Dissolve the aspic, coat the foie-gras thinly. Mix half the mayonnaise sauce with the aspic while it is still liquid. Coat the foie-gras shapes with this, and put the remainder in a mortar with the trimmings of foie-gras and pound till smooth. Season to taste, dissolve about a ¼ of an ounce of gelatine in the Béchamel sauce, add this to the pounded foie-gras, and pass all through a fine sieve. Coat the pieces of foie-gras with this mixture, set them in the moulds, fill up with more purée, smooth over with a knife, and place on the ice to set. When ready for serving, immerse the moulds quickly in tepid water, then wipe with a cloth, turn out the shapes, and dish up neatly, garnish with chopped set aspic jelly and tiny sprigs of small cress.

Allow 1 fleurette for each person.

GRAPE-FRUIT.

Grape-fruit are sometimes substituted for hors d'œuvres.

Select some nice sound, ripe fruit, wipe carefully, cut them in halves. Take out the pips and core and loosen the fruit from the skin. Cut the fruit into suitable small pieces, but leave the pieces as if uncut in the halved skin.

The syrup should be drained off, sweetened to taste and, if liked, flavoured with a little sherry, and poured over the fruit again.

Serve on a glass hors d'œuvre dish accompanied by a teaspoon and decorated with angelica. Keep on the ice until required.

HERRING FILLETS À LA DUBOIS.

Procure some preserved fillets de hareng (herring fillets), 2 ripe firm tomatoes, French olives, 1 hard-boiled egg and some cress.

Drain the fillets on a cloth. Peel and slice the tomatoes, and lay them on the bottom of a glass or other hors d'œuvre dish. Arrange the herring fillets upon these, chop some stoned French olives and yolk and white of hard-boiled egg, and place these tastefully in alternate rows upon the fillets. Garnish with tiny sprigs of cress and serve.

Allow 1 or 2 fillets to each person.

HERRING ROLLS. (Paupiettes de Harengs.)

Have ready 4 salt herrings, 3 filleted anchovies, a pinch of cayenne, two hard-boiled eggs, 1 lemon, 1½ oz. of butter, parsley, beetroot and gherkins.

Steep the herrings in cold water for a few hours; fillet them, removing the white skin and all bones; cut each lengthwise in two and pare neatly. Put the trimmings of the fillet into a mortar, together with the anchovies, and pound till smooth; add the yolks of the hard-boiled eggs and the butter, season to taste (no salt), and mix thoroughly. Rub this through a fine sieve with a layer of the purée; roll up neatly. Dip the ends into finely-chopped hard-boiled white of egg. Dish up, sprinkle over some lemon-juice, garnish with thinly-cut slices of lemon, gherkin, beetroot and parsley. Serve cold.

Allow 1 roll for each person.

INDIAN PINEAPPLE SALAD. (Salade d'Ananas à l'Indienne.)

With 1 small pineapple take 1 sour apple, 2 heads of white barb, some mayonnaise sauce (p. 122), truffle and pimiento.

Peel the pineapple and cut it into slices. Peel and core the apple, cut into fine shreds, also prepare the barb, and cut it into fine strips. Mix these three together and add enough mayonnaise sauce to dress them. Place them in a glass bowl and garnish the top with thinly-cut slices of truffle, pimiento, and fine sprigs of white barb. Keep the salad on ice until required for table.

This should be sufficient for 6 or more persons.

LAX À L'HUILE WITH CUCUMBER.

To 1 tin of lax (smoked salmon preserved in oil), allow 1 tablespoonful of sweet oil, pepper and salt, 3 or 4 slices of brown bread, butter, 1 teaspoonful of chopped parsley, 1 medium-sized cucumber, 1 dessertspoonful of Orleans vinegar, 1 handful of mustard and cress and a few sprigs of watercress.

Cut the cucumber into 1½-inch pieces as near as possible of the same size. Cut the rind so as to form stripes of green and white (crinkled). Scoop out some of the centre, and round off the bottom of each so as to give them the appearance of cups. Chop the pulp scooped out of the centre, and put it in a basin, with the oil, vinegar, and chopped parsley. Stamp out some rounds of bread with a 2-inch cutter, butter them on one side, cover the buttered side with thin slices of preserved lax; cut some of the lax into fine strips, and mix with the cucumber pulp; season with pepper and salt. Put the cucumber cups on the prepared rounds of bread, and fill the cavities with the above mixture. Range them neatly on a round dish in the shape of a crown. Season the mustard and cress, etc., and arrange it tastefully in the centre of the dish.

Allow 1 cup-shape for each person.

MELON. (Melon Cantaloup.)

There are various kinds of melon served as hors d'œuvre, the cantaloup and English rock melon being the most favoured. They must not be over-ripe, and should be served as fresh as possible, and above all, very cold.

During the hot summer weather some crushed or shaved ice is usually put round the dish on which the slices of melon are served.

MELON CANTALOUP AU MARASQUIN.

Procure 1 or more cantaloup or rock melons and some Maraschino liqueur.

Cut the fruit in half, and put it into a glass bowl or deep dish, place it on another (flat) dish surrounded with crushed ice. Pour about a tablespoonful of Maraschino liqueur in each half melon, then serve as hors d'œuvre.

If small cantaloup melons are used a half is usually allowed to each person.

OLIVE SANDWICHES.

Have ready some olives, cream, pepper and thin slices of brown or white bread and butter.

Stone, chop and pound the olives finely, adding a little cream from time to time. Season to taste with pepper, pass through a fine sieve, and spread rather thickly on bread and butter. Cover with slices of bread and butter, press firmly, trim away the crusts, and divide them into triangles or squares. Serve garnished with cress or parsley.

OLIVES.

Both Spanish and French olives are suitable for hors d'œuvres, the Spanish being the most esteemed. They should remain on the table until the dessert is served. It is claimed that olives destroy the taste of what has been previously eaten, hence they are so popular as a relish. Choose them firm, and a nice green colour. Steep them in cold water before serving, dish up on small dishes or boats with a little cold water. Never use a metal fork or spoon to dress them. Those left over from a meal should be re-bottled at once with salted water, otherwise they will turn black.

OLIVES À LA MADRAS.

Have ready some Spanish olives, 9 anchovy fillets, 2 hard-boiled eggs, ½ a teaspoonful of chutney, 1 dessertspoonful of anchovy sauce or paste, 1 oz. of butter, cayenne and salt, parsley and 9 fried-bread croûtes, or rounds of biscuit fried in butter.

Stone the olives, pound in a mortar the butter, anchovy paste, yolks of egg, chutney, seasoning, and rub them through a sieve. Spread a little of the purée on each croûte, and put a stoned olive filled with the sauce purée on each. Decorate with coral and chopped white of egg. Curl an anchovy fillet round the base of each olive, dish up, garnish with parsley, and serve.

This should be sufficient for 9 persons.

OLIVES À LA TARTARE.

Take a few slices of brown bread, 1 gill of stiff tartare sauce (p. 124), ½ a gill of aspic jelly, 6 Spanish olives, 6 shrimp or prawn tails and a few sprigs of parsley.

Stamp out 6 rounds of stale brown bread with a 1½-inch

cutter. Thoroughly incorporate the aspic jelly with the tartare sauce. Dip each round of bread in the sauce to mask completely. If not satisfactory at first, coat for a second or third time. Stone the olives, fill each with tartare sauce, and place in the centre of each croûte. Dish up on little glass dishes, put a shrimp or small prawn-tail in each olive, garnish with parsley, and serve.

This should be sufficient for 6 persons.

OLIVES IN JELLY. (Olives à l'Aspic.)

Have at hand some turned olives, anchovy and watercress butter (pp. 102, and 104), croûtes of fried bread, aspic jelly and chervil.

Fill each olive with anchovy butter, and place them in small moulds previously lined with aspic jelly and decorated with chervil. Fill the moulds with cold liquid aspic jelly, and keep on ice until firm. Meanwhile spread each croûte rather thickly with watercress butter, and, when ready, place the moulds upon them.

Allow 1 mould to each person.

OLIVES ON CROÛTES. (Canapés aux Olives.)

Prepare 8 or 9 round croûtes of fried bread, and take 8 or 9 olives, some foie-gras and a few sprigs of chervil.

Remove the stones from the olives and fill the cavities with foie-gras, also spread the croûtes with the same. Decorate the top of each olive with a sprig of chervil, and place them on the croûtes.

This should be sufficient for 6 or 7 persons.

OYSTERS. (Huîtres.)

There are many ways of dressing oysters, either hot or cold, but only one way of serving them " au naturel," which is considered the most popular hors d'œuvre. Only the best kinds, natives—Whitstable or Colchester oysters, should be served " au naturel," i.e., raw. All they need, after being opened, is to be placed on the upper shell with a little of the liquor; they are then ranged on a dish, garnished with sprigs of fresh parsley, and, if possible, surrounded with shaved ice.

Some thin slices of buttered brown bread, and quarters of lemon are handed round at the same time; also Nepaul or cayenne pepper.

OYSTERS, JELLIED. (Huîtres en Gelée.)

Take 6 oysters (natives), 1 gill of aspic jelly, a few sprigs of parsley and a lemon.

Open the oysters and beard them. Put them on a plate or pie-dish to marinade in semi-liquid aspic well flavoured with oyster liquor, lemon-juice, and chopped parsley. Clean the lower (deep) shell of each oyster, put in ½ a teaspoonful of aspic jelly : upon this place a marinaded oyster, and pour over a little of the aspic so as to mask it nicely. Keep on ice until required, then dish up, garnish with slices of lemon and parsley, and serve. Should be made some time before wanted.

This should be sufficient for 5 or 6 persons. If this is the only hors d'œuvre, 3 or 4 oysters might be allowed to each person.

OYSTERS WITH CAVIARE. (Huîtres au Caviar.)

With 6 oysters take 6 teaspoonfuls of seasoned Russian or hygienic caviare, a few sprigs of parsley and some slices of lemon.

Open the oysters and remove the beards. Put 1 teaspoonful of caviare in each of the lower (deep) shells, and place the oyster on top. Garnish the dish with slices of lemon and sprigs of parsley. Keep on ice till required for table. Should be prepared some time before wanted.

This should be sufficient for 6 persons.

PLOVERS' EGGS. (Œufs de Pluvier.)

Boil the eggs for about 8 minutes, plunge them into cold water and remove the shells, or if preferred shell only the pointed end of each egg. Range them on a dish on a bed of watercress or parsley, and serve.

Allow 1 egg for each person.

PRAWNS, CROÛTES À LA TARTARE.

Take 4 small round dinner rolls, 18 large prawns (picked), 1 large gherkin, 6 anchovy fillets, white part of 1 hard-boiled egg, 1 ladleful of tartare sauce, mustard and cress, cold aspic jelly, lobster butter (p. 103) and a few sprigs of parsley.

Cut the rolls in equal halves, scoop out the crumbs and allow the crusts to dry in the oven. Mince finely together the prawns (picked), gherkin, anchovy fillets, and white of egg. Put the mixture into a basin and season with the tartare sauce. Put a little mustard and cress at the bottom of each crust and fill with the preparation. Stamp out some thin round slices of aspic jelly, cover the surface of each with a slice, and insert the head of the prawn in the centre of each, together with a little lobster butter. Ornament the edges also with lobster butter. Dish up, garnish with parsley, and serve.

This should be sufficient for 8 persons.

PRAWNS AND SHRIMPS. (Écrevisses et Crevettes.)

These make an excellent hors d'œuvre, and need no preparation, beyond being dressed neatly overlapping each other on small hors d'œuvre dishes.

As an alternative, $\frac{1}{2}$ a lemon studded with prawns, placed in the centre of a flat dish, and surrounded with prawns or pink shrimps, and garnished with parsley, makes a pretty dish.

PRAWNS IN SAVOURY JELLY. (Écrevisses en Aspic.)

Have ready some aspic jelly, lobster coral, chopped gherkins or olives, picked prawns, green butter (p. 103) and some bread.

Line some small dariole-moulds with a thin layer of aspic jelly, and when nearly set, sprinkle over with chopped lobster coral and chopped gherkins or olives. Place 2 or 3 picked prawns in each mould and fill up with aspic jelly. Put the moulds on ice to get firm. Prepare as many fried-bread croûtons (round) as there are moulds. Mask one side of each with green herb butter. Turn out the moulds and place one on the centre of each croûte. Dish up, garnish tastefully, and serve.

Allow 1 mould for each person.

RADISHES. (Radis.)

Choose small, round and firm radishes of a light red and white colour. Trim and wash them in plenty of water (the outer skins should be scraped off and the leaves cut to an inch in length). Dish up in little boats, or glass dishes, with a little cold water.

RÉMOULADE OF ARTICHOKE BOTTOMS.

With 1 dozen small preserved artichoke bottoms take ½ a pint of vegetable macédoine, some mayonnaise sauce (p. 122), finely-chopped gherkins, capers, red pimiento and olives.

Trim the artichokes neatly, add the chopped gherkins and capers to sufficient of the mayonnaise sauce to dress the vegetables, and then add to the vegetables, and fill in the hollow part of the artichoke with the mixture. Mask the surface carefully with stiff mayonnaise, and decorate with strips of red pimiento and sliced stoned olives. Dish up, and send to table.

This should be sufficient for 12 persons.

RUSSIAN CROÛTES. (Croûtes à la Russe.)

Procure 2 tablespoonfuls of finely-shredded cold smoked or spiced beef, 2 hard-boiled eggs, 1 small horseradish, 1 gill of cream (sour if possible), salad-oil, vinegar, lemon-juice, cayenne pepper and salt.

The strips of beef should be about 1 inch long and a ¼ of an inch wide; when cut, sprinkle over them 1 teaspoonful of salad-oil, vinegar and a little pepper, and let them remain for ½ an hour. Meanwhile cover each croûte with a slice of hard-boiled egg seasoned with salt and pepper; scrape the horseradish finely and stir it into the cream, which must be previously whipped and seasoned with a little cayenne and a few drops of lemon-juice. Place the strips of beef on the croûtes, piling them high in the centre, cover with the horseradish sauce, and serve.

This should be sufficient for 6 or 7 persons.

SALADS. (*See* Salad Section, p. 105.)

SANDWICHES. (*See* Sandwich Section, p. 93.)

SARDINE EGGS. (Sardines aux Œufs.)

With 4 sardines and 4 hard-boiled eggs take 2 tablespoonfuls of white sauce, 1 teaspoonful of essence of anchovy, a few sprigs of watercress, cayenne, 1 dessertspoonful of coarsely-chopped pickled gherkin, a little oil and vinegar.

Cut the eggs across in halves, trim off the extreme end of each to enable them to stand firmly, and carefully remove the yolks. Skin and bone the sardines, chop them coarsely, and pound them together with the yolks of eggs till smooth. Add the anchovy-essence and the white sauce gradually until a moist paste is obtained, then season to taste, and rub through a hair sieve. Add the gherkin to the preparation, put it into the white of egg cases, garnish with watercress seasoned with oil and vinegar, and serve.

This should be sufficient for 8 persons.

SARDINES IN ASPIC. (Sardines en Gelée.)

Take 6 or 8 sardines, cooked tongue or lax (smoked salmon preserved in oil), aspic jelly, and some thin slices of tomato, cucumber and cooked beetroot.

Drain the sardines by placing them on a cloth. Carefully remove the skins. Roll up each sardine thus prepared in a thin skin of cooked tongue or lax, whichever is preferred. Place them in a sauté-pan containing a layer of previously-set aspic jelly, pour over sufficient half-set aspic to cover the sardine rolls, and put on ice to set. Cut out the shapes as neatly as possible and range them tastefully on a dish. Garnish the dish with the slices of tomato, cucumber and cooked beetroot.

Allow 1 sardine roll for each person.

SARDINES, SMOKED. (Sardines fumées.)

Smoked sardines, also Royans and Kieler Sprotten, are of excellent flavour. This is caused by the process of smoking prior to being put in olive oil, which gives the fish a distinctive flavour. They may be served plain or treated in the same way as ordinary sardines, for which a number of recipes are given.

SHRIMPS. (*See* Prawns and Shrimps.)

SOUSED FISH. (Poissons marinés.)

Have ready some boiled fish (or other fish left over), fish stock, vinegar, a few leaves of fennel, bay-leaf, 2 cloves, 1 dozen peppercorns, 2 slices of lemon and a little salt.

Place the neatest pieces of fish in a deep dish. Boil up the fish stock with an equal quantity of vinegar, and the herbs, lemon and seasoning. Pour over the fish, turn same over gently from time to time so that the seasoning gets thoroughly saturated.

SOUSED SALMON. (Saumon mariné.)

To a medium-sized piece of boiled salmon, allow sufficient vinegar to cover the fish, 2 small bay-leaves, 4 cloves, 6 long peppercorns, 10 juniper berries, a lump of sugar, some mayonnaise or vinaigrette sauce (pp. 122 and 124), and a little salt.

Place the piece of boiled salmon that is to be soused or pickled in a deep dish; boil the vinegar, add the bay-leaves, cloves, peppercorns, juniper berries, sugar and salt. Pour the boiling vinegar over the fish, and serve when it is quite cold, whole or shredded, made up with mayonnaise or vinaigrette sauce.

SWEDISH HORS D'ŒUVRE. (Hors d'Œuvre Suédois.)

With 4 oz. of cooked cold chicken take 2 fillets of smoked herring, 1 large cold boiled potato, 3 or 4 slices of pickled beetroot, a little mayonnaise sauce (*see* p. 122), and 1 hard-boiled egg.

Cut the chicken, herring, potato, and beetroot into small slices, and season with the mayonnaise sauce. Mix well, and place on little hors d'œuvre dishes. Decorate with the finely-chopped yolk and white of hard-boiled egg.

This should be sufficient for 6 or 7 persons.

TOMATOES À LA NIÇOISE.

Take ½ a lb. of cooked salmon (free from skin and bones), ½ a gill of mayonnaise, ¼ of a gill of aspic (liquid), 4 even-sized tomatoes and some green salad.

Pound the salmon, add the mayonnaise, season and rub through a sieve, then incorporate the aspic. Cut the tomatoes into quarters, remove the pulp, and re-shape with the prepared purée. Range tastefully on a hors d'œuvre dish upon a bed of finely-shredded and seasoned green salad, and serve.

This should be sufficient for 4 persons.

TOMATOES WITH SHRIMPS. (Tomates aux Crevettes.)

With 4 medium-sized ripe tomatoes procure some picked shrimps, salt, pepper, salad dressing, cucumber and a few sprigs of parsley.

Peel the tomatoes, cut them in halves, and remove or scoop out the interior (pulp portion) of each. Fill them with a salad composed of picked shrimps, suitably seasoned with salt, pepper, and salad dressing. Place a thinly-cut slice of cucumber on the top of each, range tastefully on an hors d'œuvre dish, garnish with parsley and serve.

This should be sufficient for 8 persons.

TUNNY FISH. (Thon mariné.)

The tunny is a kind of fish which resembles the cod; it is usually obtained preserved or marinaded in oil. The flesh is very firm, has a delicate flavour, and looks very much like cooked veal. It makes a highly-esteemed hors d'œuvre, but is hardly ever served otherwise. To serve it, cut it into slices, arrange them on oblong or round glass dishes in rows overlapping one another. Ornament the sides alternately with little heaps of chopped capers and chopped parsley. Pour a little sweet oil over the fish just before sending to table.

TUNNY FISH WITH TOMATOES. (Thon aux Tomates.)

Have ready 3 small ripe tomatoes, some preserved tunny fish, oil, vinegar, seasoning and a little chopped parsley.

Peel the tomatoes by steeping them first in boiling water. Cut them into thin slices and remove the seeds. Range them in layers alternately with the preserved tunny fish on a hors d'œuvre dish. Sprinkle with chopped parsley, and pour over a little salad dressing composed of oil, vinegar and seasoning.

This should be sufficient for 6 or more persons.

ZÉPHIRES. (*See* **note under recipe for Cheese Zéphires, p. 13.**)

CHAPTER II

SAVOURIES

The Savoury forms the final course of a dinner (before the dessert), and should be made and served in very small portions—it should be a *bonne bouche*, just a mouthful.

A well-chosen savoury adds much to the success of a dinner, which epicures, and others who know how to dine, would not consider complete without.

Most savouries are served hot, but a number of dishes are served cold, especially in the summer; the number affords a boundless choice of variety, and in their preparation immense scope in design and arrangement will be found.

The most popular savouries are those made from oysters, caviare, lobster, smoked fish and cheese.

ANCHOVY AIGRETTES. (Aigrettes d'Anchois.)

Take 6 anchovies, 2 tablespoonfuls of thick white sauce (*see* **Sauces**), 1 teaspoonful of grated Parmesan cheese, essence of anchovy, cayenne, frying-batter (*see* **Oyster Fritters,** p. 53), and some frying-fat.

Wash and dry the anchovies, remove the bones, and divide them into small fillets. Mix with them the white sauce and cheese, and add anchovy essence and cayenne to taste. Drop small teaspoonfuls of the mixture into the batter, taking care to coat them completely, then fry them in hot fat until crisp and lightly browned, and drain well. Dish in a pyramidal form, sprinkle with Parmesan cheese and Krona pepper, and serve as quickly as possible.

This should be sufficient for 6 or 8 persons.

Note.—Anchovies may be obtained at any time.

ANCHOVY AND EGG FINGERS. (Canapés d'Anchois aux Œufs.)

Procure 8 or 10 anchovies, 2 hard-boiled eggs, 1 tablespoonful of finely-chopped pickled gherkin, some stale bread, butter, anchovy-essence and cayenne.

Wash, bone and dry the anchovies; rub the yolks of the eggs through a fine sieve, and chop the whites finely. Cut thin slices of stale bread into fingers, fry them in clarified butter or fat, and drain well. Add a pinch of cayenne and a few drops of anchovy-essence to a little butter, mix well, spread it on the fingers, and lay on each an anchovy. Decorate in 3 divisions, covering the centre lightly with gherkin, with the white and yolk of egg on opposite sides. Make thoroughly hot before serving.

This should be sufficient for 6 or 8 persons.

ANCHOVY CROÛTES À L'INDIENNE. (Croûtes d'Anchois à l'Indienne.)

With 8 or 10 anchovies take ½ a teaspoonful of curry-paste, 1 hard-boiled egg, a few thin slices of toast, butter, lemon-juice, Krona pepper, chopped parsley.

Bone, wash and dry the anchovies, and divide them into fillets. Chop the white of the egg finely, rub the yolk through a fine sieve, and incorporate with it the curry-paste, and as much liquid butter as necessary to mix the whole to a moist paste. Let the toast be thin and crisp, cut it into rounds or triangles, butter well, spread on the mixture, lay on each a filleted anchovy, and season with Krona pepper. Add 2 or 3 drops of lemon-juice, decorate with white of egg, sprinkle half the croûtes with Krona pepper, and the remainder with parsley. Place them in a hot oven for 3 or 4 minutes, then serve.

This should be sufficient for 6 or 8 persons.

ANCHOVY ECLAIRS. (Eclairs d'Anchois.)

Have ready 8 to 10 anchovies, some puff-paste trimmings, grated Parmesan cheese and a little milk.

The eclairs should have the appearance of miniature sausage rolls. Wash, bone and dry the anchovies. Roll the paste out thin, cut it into oblong pieces, slightly longer than the anchovies. Enclose an anchovy in each piece, seal the edge folded over with a little milk, sprinkle with cheese, and bake in a brisk oven until nicely browned and crisp. Serve hot.

This should be sufficient for 6 or 8 persons.

SAVOURIES

ANCHOVY FINGERS. (Canapés d'Anchois.)

Take 8 or 10 anchovies, ½ a teaspoonful of finely-chopped parsley, 1 finely-chopped shallot, ½ an oz. of butter, 2 or 3 pieces of buttered toast, a spoonful of lemon-juice, and a little Krona pepper and white pepper.

Bone the anchovies and wash them in warm water. Cut the toast into fingers, sprinkle them with shallot and parsley, and lay on each an anchovy. Add a few drops of lemon-juice and a seasoning of pepper, sprinkle on a little Krona pepper, place a morsel of butter on each, make hot in the oven, and serve.

This should be sufficient for 6 or 8 persons.

ANCHOVY RISSOLETTES. (Rissolettes d'Anchois.)

With 4 anchovies take 3 raw yolks of eggs, 1 whole raw egg, 1 oz. of butter, ¾ lb. short crust paste, 1 teaspoonful of grated Parmesan cheese, breadcrumbs, a few grains of cayenne and some frying-fat.

Wash, skin, bone and dry the anchovies, then chop them and rub them through a fine sieve. Steam or bake the yolks of eggs in a buttered cup or small mould, and pass them through a sieve. Melt the butter, mix with it the anchovies, yolk of eggs and cheese, adding cayenne to taste. Roll out the paste as thin as a wafer, cut it into ¾-inch diameter rounds, place on each half 1 teaspoonful of the preparation, wet the edges, and fold over into a crescent shape. Brush over with egg, coat with breadcrumbs, fry in hot fat until crisp and nicely browned, then drain well. Dish in a pyramidal form, sprinkle with Parmesan cheese and Krona pepper, and serve as hot as possible.

This should be sufficient for 6 or 8 persons.

ANCHOVY TOAST. (Croûtes d'Anchois.)

To 6 anchovies allow ½ an oz. of butter, 1 yolk of egg, 1 finely-chopped shallot, ½ a teaspoonful of finely-chopped parsley, 2 or 3 pieces of toast, butter and a few grains of cayenne pepper.

Wash and bone the anchovies, and chop them coarsely. Heat the butter in a small stewpan, fry the shallot until lightly browned, then add the anchovies, parsley and yolk of egg, and season with cayenne. Stir by the side of the fire until the mixture thickens, then pour it on the toast, previously well-buttered, and serve hot.

This should be sufficient for 6 or 8 persons.

"ANGELS ON HORSEBACK." (Les Anges à Cheval.)

Have ready 12 oysters, 12 small thin slices of bacon, 12 small round croûtes of fried bread, $\frac{1}{2}$ a teaspoonful of finely-chopped shallot, $\frac{1}{2}$ a teaspoonful of finely-chopped parsley, about a teaspoonful of lemon-juice and a seasoning of Krona pepper.

Beard the oysters, trim the bacon, cutting each piece just large enough to roll round an oyster, season with Krona pepper, sprinkle on a little shallot and parsley. Lay an oyster on each, add a few drops of lemon-juice, roll up tightly, and secure the bacon in position with a large pin. Fry in a frying-pan or bake in a hot oven just long enough to crisp the bacon (further cooking would harden the oysters), remove the pins and serve on the croûtes of fried bread.

This should be sufficient for 8 or 9 persons.

BLOATER TOAST. (Croûtes à la Yarmouth.)

Procure 2 bloaters with soft roes, $1\frac{1}{2}$ oz. of butter, 1 egg, and a little salt and cayenne, and prepare 8 squares of buttered toast.

Remove the roes, grill the bloaters, free them from skin and bone, then chop them, and rub them through a fine sieve. Heat 1 oz. of butter in a small stewpan, add the fish, and when hot put in the egg, season to taste, and stir by the side of the fire until the mixture thickens. Meanwhile divide the roes into 8 pieces, and fry them in the remainder of the butter. Spread the fish preparation on the croûtes of buttered toast, lay the roe on the top, send to table, and serve as hot as possible.

This should be sufficient for 6 or 7 persons.

CAVIARE BOUCHÉES. (*See* Caviare Patties, p. 33.)

CAVIARE PANCAKES. (Caviar de Russe aux blenis.)

Procure some Russian caviare and 1 pint of milk, 2 eggs, 4 heaped tablespoonfuls of flour, salt and dripping.

Put the flour and a good pinch of salt into a basin, make a well in the centre, break in the eggs, stir, gradually mixing in

CHEESE AND EGG DISHES

1. Cheese d'Artois. 2. Scrambled Eggs. 3. Cold Cheese Creams.

the flour from the sides, and add milk by degrees until a thick smooth batter is formed. Now beat well for 10 minutes, then add the remainder of the milk, cover, and let it stand for at least 1 hour. When ready to use, put a few small pieces of butter or good sweet dripping in a frying-pan, and while the pan and butter are getting thoroughly hot, give the batter another good beating. Pour a very thin layer of batter into the pan and fry from 2 to 3 minutes.

Make the pancakes as small and as thin as possible. Spread them with caviare, roll them tightly, and cut off the ends in a sharply-slanting direction. Serve as quickly as possible.

Allow 1 pancake to each person.

CAVIARE PATTIES. (Bouchées au Caviar.)

With 1 small pot of caviare take 2 tablespoonfuls of tomato sauce, ½ an oz. of butter, 1 finely-chopped shallot, a few drops of lemon-juice, a few sprigs of crisply-fried parsley and some puff-paste.

When the puff-paste is ready for the last turn, roll it out to about ⅓ of an inch in thickness, and stamp out 8 or 9 rounds with a hot wet cutter, 2½ inches in diameter. Brush over with beaten egg, then take a cutter 2 or 3 sizes smaller, dip it into boiling water, and make an incision in the centre of each round, to ½ the depth of the paste. Bake in a hot oven ; when done, remove and preserve the lids, scoop out the soft inside, and keep the cases hot until required. Cook the shallot slightly in the butter, then add the caviare, tomato sauce and a few drops of lemon-juice. Fill the cases with the preparation, put on the lids, garnish with crisply-fried parsley, and serve as quickly as possible.

This should be sufficient for 6 or 8 persons.

CHEESE AIGRETTES. (Aigrettes au Parmesan.)

Have ready 3 oz. of grated Parmesan cheese, 4 oz. of flour, 2 oz. of butter, 2 eggs, ½ a pint of water, a few grains of cayenne and salt to taste.

Put the butter and water into a small stewpan ; when boiling add the previously dried and sieved flour, and stir vigorously over the fire until the panada leaves the sides of the pan quite clean. Now mix in, off the fire, the cheese, the yolks of eggs, beating each one in separately, add seasoning to taste, and lastly stir in the stiffly-whisked whites of eggs.

Turn on to a plate, and when cold drop small rough pieces of it into hot fat, but they must not fry too quickly or the surface will become too brown before the interior is sufficiently cooked. On the other hand, if the fat is too cold it soaks into the paste, and the aigrettes are greasy. As the success of this dish depends chiefly on the frying, the greatest possible care should be bestowed upon it. After being well drained the aigrettes are usually arranged in a pyramidal form on a folded napkin or dish-paper, and sprinkled with Parmesan cheese or Krona pepper.

This should be sufficient for 6 or 7 persons.

CHEESE BALLS. (Boules au Fromage.)

Take 2 oz. of grated Cheshire or Cheddar cheese, 1 oz. of flour, 1 egg, salt, pepper, a few grains of cayenne and some frying-fat.

Mix the cheese, flour, and yolk of egg together, add salt, pepper, and cayenne to taste, then whisk the white of the egg to a stiff froth and stir it lightly into the rest of the ingredients. Have ready a deep pan of hot fat, drop in the mixture in teaspoonfuls and fry until nicely browned. Drain well, and dish in a pyramidal form on a folded napkin or dish-paper.

This should be sufficient for 6 or 7 persons.

CHEESE BISCUITS. (Biscuits au Fromage.)

To 12 water biscuits allow 2 tablespoonfuls of grated Cheshire or Cheddar cheese, butter, and a seasoning of white pepper and Krona pepper.

Spread the biscuits with butter, sprinkle them liberally with cheese, season well with white pepper, and, if convenient, add also a little Krona pepper. Place the biscuits in a moderate oven until the cheese melts, then serve them as quickly as possible.

This should be sufficient for 5 or 6 persons.

CHEESE BISCUITS WITH CREAM. (*See* **Recipe in Hors d'Œuvre Section,** p. 12.)

CHEESE SAVOURIES. (*See* **Chapter of Cheese and Cheese Savouries,** pp. 71–78.)

CHEESE TOASTED. (See **Recipe,** p. 78.)

Note.—See also recipes in Cheese chapter, p. 71.

SAVOURIES

CHICKENS' LIVERS, DEVILLED.

Have ready 4 chickens' livers, 3 croûtes of fried bread, bacon, finely-chopped shallot, ½ a teaspoonful of finely-chopped parsley, cayenne, pepper and salt.

Wash and dry the livers, cut them in halves, and sprinkle them well with shallot, parsley, cayenne and pepper; these ingredients should be previously mixed together. Cut some very thin slices of bacon, just large enough to roll round the liver, wrap them round tightly, and fasten them in position by means of large pins. Bake in a moderate oven for 7 or 8 minutes, then remove the pins, and dish on the croûtes.

This should be sufficient for 6 or 7 persons.

COD'S LIVER MINCED AND BAKED.

Procure ½ a lb. of cod's liver, 12 sauce oysters, ¼ of a pint of white sauce, butter, breadcrumbs, salt and pepper.

Parboil the liver and cut it into small pieces. Blanch the oysters in their own liquor, which afterwards strain and add to the white sauce. Halve or quarter the oysters, mix them with the prepared liver, and season to taste. Place in buttered scallop shells, add a little sauce, cover lightly with breadcrumbs, and on the top place 2 or 3 small pieces of butter. Bake in a moderately hot oven for 10 or 15 minutes.

This should be sufficient for 5 or 6 scallops.

COD'S LIVER QUENELLES.

Take ½ a lb. of cod's liver, 2 tablespoonfuls of breadcrumbs, 1 teaspoonful of finely-chopped parsley, the yolk of 1 egg, a little milk, salt and pepper.

Wash and dry the liver, chop it finely, and mix with it the breadcrumbs and parsley. Add sufficient milk and the yolk of an egg to bind the whole together, taking care not to make the mixture too moist. Season to taste, shape into quenelles; to do this it is necessary to use 2 dessertspoons. Dip 1 spoon into boiling water, fill it with the mixture, press it from the sides and raise it in the centre with a knife dipped in hot water, making it a nice oval shape; take another spoon, dip it into hot water, scoop the mixture from the first spoon into the second, and place in a buttered sauté-pan Poach until firm, 10 to 15 minutes, and serve with a suitable sauce.

This should be sufficient for 5 or 6 persons.

COD'S ROE. (Laitance de Cabillaud.)

Have ready ½ lb. of cod's roe, some melted butter, or other white sauce (*see* **Sauces**), a little milk or cream, brown breadcrumbs, salt and vinegar

Wash and wipe the cod's roe, and boil for about 10 minutes in water with a little salt and vinegar. Cut into dice, and put into some melted butter sauce or other white sauce diluted with a little cream or milk. Butter 4 or 5 small scallop shells, put in the roe, cover with brown breadcrumbs, and brown in the oven, or serve it on small fancy-shaped pieces of hot buttered toast.

This should be sufficient for 3 or 4 persons.

COD'S ROE CROQUETTES. (Croquettes de Laitance de Cabillaud.)

With 1 lb. of cod's roe, take ¼ of a pint of milk, 1 oz. of butter, 1 dessertspoonful of flour, 2 tablespoonfuls of mashed potato, 1 tablespoonful of breadcrumbs, 1 dessertspoonful of finely-chopped parsley, ½ a teaspoonful of finely-chopped shallot or onion, ½ a teaspoonful of powdered mixed herbs, 2 eggs, about 2 tablespoonfuls of breadcrumbs, frying-fat, and a few sprigs of fried parsley.

Boil the roe as in the preceding recipe, and when cold chop it coarsely. Melt the butter in a stewpan, fry the shallot slightly, stir in the flour, add the milk, boil for a few minutes, then put in the potato, 1 tablespoonful of breadcrumbs, the roe, parsley, herbs, and 1 egg. Season well with salt and pepper, stir over the fire until the mixture becomes thoroughly hot and the egg sufficiently cooked, then spread on a plate to cool. When ready to use, shape the croquettes in the form of corks or balls, brush them over with beaten egg, cover with breadcrumbs, and fry in hot fat until nicely browned. Drain and serve garnished with fried parsley.

This should be sufficient for 7 or 8 persons.

COD'S ROE CROÛTES. (Croûtes de Laitance de Cabillaud.)

To ½ a lb. of smoked cod's roe allow 8 oval-shaped croûtes of fried bread, 1 oz. of butter, ½ a teaspoonful of finely-chopped chives or shallot, ½ a teaspoonful of finely-chopped parsley and a little pepper and cayenne.

Soak the roe in water for 1 hour to soften it, then drain and dry it thoroughly. Heat the butter in a sauté- or frying-pan, cut the roe into 8 slices, and fry them lightly on both sides. Sprinkle the croûtes of fried bread with shallot, parsley and pepper, lay a slice of roe on each, add a few grains of cayenne, and serve as hot as possible. A more elaborate appearance may be given to the dish by decorating the roes with strips of gherkin and hard-boiled white of egg, or with some anchovy butter.

This should be sufficient for 6 or 7 persons.

Note.—Fresh roe also may be dressed in this manner. It should first be well washed, then covered with boiling water, seasoned with a dessertspoonful of vinegar, and ½ a teaspoonful of salt, boiled gently for 10 minutes, and when cold cut into slices, and cooked as directed above.

COD'S ROE FRIED. (Laitance de Cabillaud frite.)

Have ready 1 lb. of cod's roe, 1 dessertspoonful of vinegar, 1 small onion, 4 peppercorns, a bouquet-garni (parsley, thyme, bay-leaf), 1 egg, breadcrumbs, salt, frying-fat, and a few sprigs of fried parsley.

Well wash the roe in salt and water, then put it into a stewpan with the onion sliced, vinegar, ½ a teaspoonful of salt, boiling water to cover, and simmer gently for about 1½ hours. When cold, cut into thick slices, coat with egg and breadcrumbs, and fry in hot fat in a frying-pan, or in a deep pan of hot fat, until nicely browned. Drain well, garnish with fried parsley, and serve.

This should be sufficient for 6 or 7 persons.

CRAB, DEVILLED. (Crabe à la Diable.)

Have ready a medium-sized boiled crab, breadcrumbs, 1 teaspoonful of mixed mustard, 1 teaspoonful of Worcester sauce, 1 tablespoonful of oiled butter, cayenne and salt to taste and a little cream or milk.

Remove the meat from the shell and claws, clean the shell, and put it aside. Chop the meat of the crab, add to it an equal quantity of breadcrumbs, the mustard, sauce, butter, and a very liberal seasoning of cayenne and salt. Mix well, if necessary moisten with a little milk or cream, then turn the whole into the prepared shell. Cover lightly with breadcrumbs, add a few small pieces of butter, and brown in a moderately hot oven.

This should be sufficient for 4 or 5 persons.

CRAB, DRESSED.

To 1 medium-sized crab, allow 1 hard-boiled egg, 2 tablespoonfuls of vinegar, 2 tablespoonfuls of salad-oil, cayenne, and a little salt and pepper

Empty the shells, mix the meat with the vinegar and salad-oil, and season well with cayenne, salt and pepper. Clean the large shell, put in the mixture and garnish with slices of lemon, parsley, and egg, the yolk rubbed through a wire sieve and the white coarsely-chopped.

This should be sufficient for 3 or 4 persons.

CRAB, DRESSED. (Another Method.)

Take 1 medium-sized crab, 3 tablespoonfuls of salad-oil, 2 tablespoonfuls of vinegar, breadcrumbs, and a little pepper and salt. For garnishing : lobster coral, butter, hard-boiled egg, or parsley.

Pick the meat from the shell, flake it into small shreds, and add to it the same proportion of finely-grated breadcrumbs. Season to taste with pepper and salt, then mix well with the oil, and lastly the vinegar. Carefully wash and dry the shell and put in the mixture, garnishing with lobster coral, butter, or hard-boiled egg and parsley.

This should be sufficient for 4 persons.

CRAB, SCALLOPED. (Crabe en Coquille.)

Procure 2 crabs (medium-sized), and have ready a little white sauce, vinegar, breadcrumbs, butter, salt, pepper and some mustard.

Remove the meat from the claws and body, taking care to leave the unwholesome part near the head. Add about half its bulk in fine breadcrumbs, season to taste with salt, pepper and mustard, and stir in a few drops of vinegar. Add white sauce until the right consistency is obtained, then turn into buttered scallop shells, and sprinkle the surface lightly with breadcrumbs. Place small pieces of butter on the top, and bake in a moderate oven until nicely browned.

This should be sufficient for 8 or 9 scallops.

EGGS, SCRAMBLED, WITH ANCHOVIES. (Œufs brouillés aux Anchois.)

Procure 3 eggs, 3 anchovies, $\frac{3}{4}$ of an oz. of butter, 1 tablespoonful of cream or milk, ½ a teaspoonful of essence of anchovy, toast, butter, capers, parsley, pepper and salt.

Skin and bone the anchovies, and cut them into fine strips. Cut the toast into pieces 3 inches long and 2 inches wide, and spread them thickly with butter. Beat the eggs slightly, then put them with the butter, cream, and anchovy-essence into the stewpan, and season to taste. Stir by the side of the fire until the mixture thickens, put it on the toast, lay the strips of anchovy across, forming a lattice, and place a caper in each division. Re-heat in the oven, then serve garnished with parsley.

This should be sufficient for 5 or 6 persons.

EGGS STUFFED WITH PRAWNS. (Œufs farcis aux Crevettes.)

With 4 hard-boiled eggs take 12 large or 18 small prawns, 3 Gorgona anchovies, 1½ oz. of butter, ¼ of a pint of Tomato sauce (p. 124), 1 tablespoonful of Béchamel sauce (p. 121), grated Parmesan cheese, cayenne and a little salt and pepper.

Cut the eggs across in halves, cut off their extreme ends so that they may stand firmly, and remove the yolks. Put the boned anchovies and the picked prawns into a mortar, add the yolks of the eggs, pound these ingredients until smooth, then rub through a fine wire sieve. Replace in the mortar, incorporate the butter and Béchamel sauce, season to taste, then fill the cases. Sprinkle the surface with grated Parmesan cheese, place a prawn head in the centre of each, and bake in a hot oven for about 10 minutes. Serve the tomato sauce poured round the base of the dish.

This should be sufficient for 6 or 7 persons.

Note.—Strictly speaking, the gastronomic rule does not admit egg preparations to be served as after-dinner savouries, but many persons like them, and a number of other suitable recipes will be found in the chapter devoted to Eggs, p. 79.

FOIE-GRAS MEDALLIONS. (Médaillons de Foie-Gras.)

Have ready 1 terrine of foie-gras, panada, 1 white of egg, a little cream, salt and pepper, brown sauce, croûtes of toasted bread. For garnish : asparagus points cooked, strips of truffle, and hard-boiled white of egg.

Slice the foie-gras and cut it into rounds of equal size.

Chop the trimmings finely, add to them an equal quantity of panada, and pound well, adding the white of egg, a good seasoning of salt and pepper, and a little cream. Pass through a fine sieve, spread smoothly on one side of the foie-gras medallions, and steam or poach them gently for 20 minutes. Place them on the croûtes, garnish tastefully with strips of truffle and egg interlaced, and serve with the sauce poured round the medallions.

This should be sufficient for 4 or 5 persons.

FOIE-GRAS TOAST. (Croûtes de Foie-Gras.)

Procure some foie-gras, salt and pepper and prepare a few croûtes of toasted bread.

Slice the foie-gras, and stamp it into rounds, the same size as the croûtes. Warm them between 2 plates over a saucepan of boiling water, place them on the hot croûtes, season with salt and pepper, then serve.

Allow 1 croûte to each person, and 1 or 2 over.

GOLDEN BUCK.

With ¼ of a lb. of Cheshire or Cheddar cheese (preferably the former) take 2 or 3 tablespoonfuls of ale, ½ a teaspoonful of Worcester or other cruet sauce, ½ a teaspoonful of lemon-juice, 2 eggs, celery-salt, Krona pepper, 2 or 3 pieces of toast and butter.

Chop the cheese finely, put it into a stewpan, with ½ an oz. of butter and the ale, and stir vigorously until creamy, then add the Worcester sauce, lemon-juice, and the eggs previously beaten. Season to taste with celery-salt and Krona pepper, and continue stirring briskly until the mixture thickens. Trim the toast, butter well, cut each slice into 4 squares, arrange them compactly on a hot dish, and pour the cheese preparation on to them. Send to table, and serve as hot as possible.

This should be sufficient for 6 or 7 persons.

HAM AND RICE CROQUETTES. (Croquettes de Jambon au Riz.)

To ½ a lb. of finely-chopped cooked ham allow ¼ of a lb. of cooked rice, 1 oz. of butter, 3 tablespoonfuls of White sauce (see **Sauces**), 1 finely-chopped shallot, powdered sage, fried parsley, salt and pepper, 1 yolk of egg, 1 whole egg, breadcrumbs and some frying-fat.

Dry the rice well after cooking it, and chop it finely. Fry the shallot in the butter until lightly browned, then add the ham, rice, and a good pinch of sage, season with salt and pepper, and stir over the fire until hot. Now put in the white sauce and the yolk of egg mixed together, stir until the preparation thickens, then spread it on a plate. When cool shape into balls or corks, coat with egg and breadcrumbs, and fry in hot fat until nicely browned. Drain well, and serve garnished with fried parsley.

This should be sufficient for 5 or 6 persons.

HAM CROÛTES. (Croûtes au Jambon.)

Take 6 oz. of finely-chopped cooked ham, ½ an oz. of butter, 1 tablespoonful of cream, 2 yolks of eggs, 1 finely-chopped shallot, ½ a teaspoonful of finely-chopped parsley, pepper and 8 round croûtes of fried bread.

Fry the shallot in the butter until slightly browned, then add the ham and stir over the fire until hot. Now put in the yolks of eggs and cream, season with pepper, stir until the mixture thickens, then dish on the fried bread croûtes and serve sprinkled with parsley.

This should be sufficient for 6 or 7 persons.

HAM RAMAKINS.

Procure 5 oz. of finely-chopped lean cooked ham, 2 eggs, 4 tablespoonfuls of milk, ½ a teaspoonful of powdered mixed herbs, made mustard, Krona pepper, salt and pepper.

Beat the yolks of eggs slightly, add the ham, milk, herbs, a small ½ mustardspoonful of mustard, salt and pepper to taste, and mix well together. Have ready 8 well-buttered china ramakin cases, fill them rather more than three-quarters full with the mixture, and bake until set. Meanwhile beat the white of egg to a stiff froth, season with a little salt, and pile roughly above the level of the cases. Sprinkle with Krona pepper, replace in the oven and bake until the white of egg is crisp and lightly browned. Serve hot.

This should be sufficient for 5 or 6 persons.

SAVOURIES

HERRING ROE CROÛTES. (Croûtes de Laitance de Harengs.)

Have ready 8 fresh soft roes, some anchovy paste, toast, butter, 2 lemons, fried parsley and cayenne.

Cut the toast into round or oval-shaped pieces, butter them liberally, and spread them lightly with anchovy-paste. Melt about 1 oz. of butter in a sauté- or frying-pan, and shake or gently toss the roes in it over the fire until lightly browned. Dish on the prepared toast, sprinkle with lemon-juice and cayenne, garnish with slices of lemon and crisply-fried parsley, and serve as hot as possible.

This should be sufficient for 6 or 7 persons.

Note.—Tinned roes are less expensive, and although their flavour is inferior to that of fresh roes, they answer very well for ordinary purposes. As they are already cooked, they simply require re-heating.

HERRING ROE TIT-BITS. (Bonnes Bouches de Laitance de Harengs.)

Take 4 fresh soft roes, bacon, 8 round croûtes of fried bread or buttered toast, anchovy paste, fine strips of pickled gherkin, Krona pepper, lemon-juice and salt.

Divide the roes in half, fold each half in two, and cut some very thin slices of bacon just large enough to roll round the roe. Sprinkle the inside of each piece of bacon with lemon-juice, Krona pepper and salt, then fold them lightly round the roe and secure the bacon in position with a large pin. Fry in a sauté-pan or bake in a quick oven until nicely browned and crisp. Meanwhile spread the croûtes thinly with anchovy paste, add a few strips of gherkin, cover with a buttered paper, and heat in the oven. When ready to serve, remove the pins, sprinkle with Krona pepper, dish on the croûtes, and send them to table as hot as possible.

This should be sufficient for 6 or 7 persons.

HERRING ROES, BAKED. (Laitance de Harengs au gratin.)

With 8 fresh soft roes take 3 tablespoonfuls of thick brown sauce (p. 121), 1 tablespoonful of lemon-juice, a few drops of anchovy-essence, 1½ oz. of butter, 4 coarsely-chopped button mushrooms, 1 very finely-chopped shallot, ½ a teaspoonful of finely-chopped parsley, lightly-browned breadcrumbs and 8 round or oval china or paper soufflé-cases.

Brush the inside of the cases with clarified butter. Heat 1 oz. of butter in a small stewpan, put in the mushrooms, shallot and parsley, fry lightly, then drain off the butter into a sauté-pan. Add the brown sauce, lemon-juice and anchovy-essence to the mushrooms, etc., season to taste, and when hot pour a small teaspoonful into each paper case. Re-heat the butter in the sauté-pan, toss the roes gently over the fire until lightly browned, then place one in each case, and cover them with the remainder of the sauce. Add a thin layer of breadcrumbs, on the top place 2 or 3 morsels of butter, and bake in a quick oven for a few minutes. Serve as hot as possible.

This should be sufficient for 6 or 7 persons.

IRISH RABBIT OR RAREBIT.

Procure 4 oz. of Cheshire or Cheddar cheese, $\frac{1}{2}$ an oz. of butter, 2 or 3 tablespoonfuls of milk, 1 dessertspoonful of coarsely-chopped pickled gherkin, some vinegar, made mustard and pepper to taste and some pieces of hot buttered toast.

Put the butter, milk and cheese cut into small pieces into a saucepan, stir by the side of the fire until the ingredients become creamy, then add vinegar, made mustard and pepper to taste, and lastly the gherkin. Have ready some squares of hot well-buttered toast, pour on the preparation, and serve quickly.

This should be sufficient for 6 or 7 persons.

KIDNEY TOAST. (Rognons sur Croûtes.)

Take 2 sheep's kidneys, or $\frac{1}{2}$ a lb. of bullock's kidney, 1 oz. of butter, $\frac{1}{2}$ a teaspoonful of lemon-juice, cayenne, pepper, salt and 2 slices of hot buttered toast.

Stew the kidneys in a little stock or water until tender, remove the skin and gristle, and pound them in a mortar until quite smooth. Add the butter, lemon-juice, a good pinch of cayenne, and salt and pepper to taste, and pass the mixture through a wire sieve. Spread lightly on the prepared toast, make thoroughly hot in the oven, then serve.

This should be sufficient for 4 or 5 persons.

KIDNEY TOAST À LA MADRAS. (Croûtes de Rognons à la Madras.)

With 2 sheep's kidneys take 4 small rounds of buttered toast, curry-paste, $\frac{1}{4}$ of a teaspoonful of grated lemon-rind, 1 egg, breadcrumbs, butter, salt and pepper.

Skin the kidneys, cut them in halves lengthwise, run small skewers through them to keep them flat, and season them with salt, pepper, and a few grains of cayenne. Mix the lemon-rind and a little salt and pepper with the egg, dip in the kidneys, and roll them in breadcrumbs. Have ready a little hot butter in a frying-pan, and fry them lightly and quickly, cooking the cut side first. Trim the toast to a size slightly larger than $\frac{1}{2}$ a kidney, spread with a thin layer of curry-paste, dish the kidneys upon them, and serve as hot as possible.

This should be sufficient for 4 persons.

KIDNEYS AND OYSTERS.

Grill 2 or 3 sheep's kidneys (*see* recipe for **Kidneys, Grilled,** below), oysters, salt and pepper and some croûtes of toasted bread.

Blanch the oysters in their own liquor, taking care that they are not over-cooked. Place 2 on the top of each half of grilled kidney, season lightly with salt and pepper, and serve on the croûtes of toasted bread.

This should be sufficient for 4 or 5 persons.

KIDNEYS, GRILLED. (Rognons Grillés.)

Have ready kidneys, croûtons of fried bread or toast, salad-oil or oiled butter, and Maître d'hôtel butter (p. 104).

Cover the kidneys with boiling water, and let them remain in it for 2 minutes. Drain, dry, remove the skin, split in two length-wise, but without detaching the halves. Pass a steel skewer through them, to keep them open, brush over with salad-oil or oiled butter, season with salt and pepper, and grill them over a clear fire, cooking the cut side first. Time required for cooking depends upon the size of the kidney and individual taste; 5 minutes will be found sufficient for a small kidney, and 8 minutes for a large one. Have the croûtons ready and as hot as possible, place a kidney on each with a small pat of Maître d'hôtel butter in the centre of each kidney. Serve at once.

SAVOURIES

LOBSTER, BAKED. (Homard au gratin.)

To 1 medium-sized lobster allow 1½ oz. of butter, 2 or 3 tablespoonfuls of white sauce, 1 egg, the juice of ½ a lemon, 1 dessertspoonful of finely-chopped parsley, ½ a teaspoonful of finely-chopped shallots, brown breadcrumbs, nutmeg, salt and pepper.

Cut the lobster in two lengthwise, remove the meat from the shells, and mince it coarsely. Melt the butter in a stewpan, fry the shallots for 2 or 3 minutes without browning, then add the lobster, white sauce, parsley, lemon-juice, a pinch of nutmeg, as well as salt and pepper to taste; then stir over the fire until thoroughly hot. Beat the egg slightly, add it to the mixture, and cook until it begins to bind. Have ready the two halves of the large shell, put in the mixture, cover lightly with brown breadcrumbs, put 3 or 4 very small pieces of butter on the top, and bake for 10 or 15 minutes in a moderate oven. Garnish with fried parsley.

This should be sufficient for 5 or 6 persons.

Note.—Lobsters are obtainable all the year round, but are at their best from July to September.

LOBSTER COQUILLES. (Coquilles de Homard.)

Have ready 1 medium-sized lobster, mushrooms, butter, White sauce (p. 124), salt, pepper, nutmeg, short crust paste and a few sprigs of parsley.

Line some small shell-shaped moulds with light paste crust. After pricking the paste with a fork fill the lined moulds with uncooked rice or dried peas, and bake them in a moderate oven a golden-brown. When done, take out the rice or peas, and place the pastry shells on a sieve. Cut the meat of the lobster (preserved lobster of a reliable brand will do) into small dice, put it in a stewpan with some chopped mushrooms and butter, allowing 8 mushrooms and ½ an oz. of butter to every ½ lb. of lobster. Stir over the fire until thoroughly hot, then moisten, with white sauce. Season with pepper, salt, a little grated nutmeg, and a pinch of cayenne. Keep the mixture hot in a bain-marie so that it is ready for use when required. Warm the baked shells in the oven, fill them with the mixture, strew over a little red panurette (a preparation of grated rusks, used instead of lobster coral for decoration), or some fried breadcrumbs; the former, however, makes the shells more effective. Dish up on small plates, and garnish with a sprig or two of parsley. A little anchovy-essence added to the mixture will improve the flavour.

This should be sufficient for 8 persons.

LOBSTER, CREAMED. (Homard à la Newbury.)

With 1 small lobster take 1 oz. of butter, 2 yolks of eggs, ½ a gill of thick cream, a few drops of lemon-juice, ½ a teaspoonful of salt, 1 saltspoonful of Krona pepper, a pinch of nutmeg and a few sprigs of parsley, and prepare 7 or 8 small croûtes of fried or toasted bread.

Chop the flesh of the lobster finely, cook it in the butter for 6 or 7 minutes, stirring meanwhile, then add the yolks of eggs and cream, previously mixed together, and the seasoning. Stir by the side of the fire until the mixture thickens, then dish it on the fried or toasted bread croûtes, garnish with parsley, and serve hot.

This should be sufficient for 6 or 7 persons.

LOBSTER CROQUETTES. (Croquettes de Homard.)

Take 1 medium-sized lobster (or a good brand of tinned lobster), 1 oz. of butter, 1 tablespoonful of flour, 1 tablespoonful of cream or milk, 1 whole egg, 1 yolk of egg, salt and pepper to taste, cayenne, panurette (grated rusks) or breadcrumbs, frying-fat and a few sprigs of crisply fried parsley.

Chop the flesh of the lobster finely. Melt the butter in a stewpan, stir in the flour, add rather less than a gill of cold water, and boil well. Now put in the lobster, cream or milk, a pinch of cayenne, salt and pepper to taste, stir over the fire until thoroughly hot, then add the yolk of 1 egg. When the mixture begins to thicken spread it on a plate to cool, and when ready to use shape it in the form of cutlets or corks. Brush these over well with egg, coat with panurette (this preparation, which resembles exceedingly fine red breadcrumbs, is sold in packets), and fry a golden-brown in hot fat. Drain well, arrange neatly on a folded napkin or dishpaper, garnish with fried parsley, and serve.

This should be sufficient for 5 or 6 persons.

LOBSTER CUTLETS.

Have ready 1 large lobster, 1½ oz. of butter, 1 oz. of flour, ¼ of a pint of milk or water, 1 tablespoonful of cream, 1 egg, breadcrumbs, salt, cayenne, parsley and frying-fat.

SAVOURIES

Remove the flesh from the lobster, and chop it into small pieces. Pound the spawn (if any) with ½ an oz. of butter, and pass it through a hair sieve. Melt 1 oz. of butter in a small stewpan, stir in the flour, add the milk, and boil well. Then add to it the lobster, cream, spawn, cayenne, and salt, mix well together, and turn on to a plate to cool. When the mixture is firm enough to mould, make it up into small cutlets, cover them with egg and breadcrumb, and fry until nicely browned in hot fat. Dish in a circle, putting a piece of lobster feeler in each cutlet to represent a bone, and garnish with fried parsley.

This should be sufficient for 9 or 10 small cutlets.

LOBSTER DEVILLED.

Take 1 lobster, 3 tablespoonfuls of white breadcrumbs, a few browned breadcrumbs, 1½ oz. of butter, 2 tablespoonfuls of white sauce, or cream, cayenne.

Cut the lobster in two lengthwise, remove and chop the meat finely. Melt the butter, pour it on the lobster, add the white breadcrumbs, and the sauce, season rather highly with cayenne, and mix well. Press the mixture lightly into the lobster shell, cover with browned breadcrumbs, put 3 or 4 pieces of butter on the top, and bake for about 20 minutes in a moderate oven. Serve hot or cold.

LOBSTER, DEVILLED, SUR CROÛTES. (Croûtes de Homard à la Diable.)

To 1 small lobster allow 1 tablespoonful of breadcrumbs, 1 oz. of butter, 1 teaspoonful of white wine vinegar, a few drops of tarragon vinegar, a few drops of lemon juice, 1 mustardspoonful of made mustard, a little cayenne, nutmeg, Krona pepper, 2 or 3 tablespoonfuls of thick cream or Béchamel sauce (p. 121), and 7 or 8 croûtes of fried bread.

Pound the flesh of the lobster with the breadcrumbs, butter and vinegar in a mortar until smooth, then rub through a sieve. Season highly with pepper and cayenne, add the mustard and a pinch of nutmeg, and, if needed, moisten with more vinegar. Pile the preparation on the fried bread croûtes, cover with whipped cream or Béchamel sauce seasoned with cayenne and lemon, sprinkle with Krona pepper and serve.

This should be sufficient for 6 or 7 persons.

LOBSTER RISSOLES.

With 1 small lobster take some puff-paste trimmings, 1 yolk of egg, 1 or 2 tablespoonfuls of white sauce or fish sauce, $\frac{1}{2}$ a teaspoonful of finely-chopped parsley, cayenne, egg and breadcrumbs and some frying-fat.

Remove the flesh of the lobster from the shell, and chop it finely. Put it into a saucepan with the yolk of egg, white sauce, parsley, and a pinch of cayenne, and stir over the fire until thoroughly hot. Season to taste, turn it on to a plate, and put aside until cold. Roll the paste out as thinly as possible, stamp out into rounds about 2 inches in diameter, and place a little of the lobster preparation in the centre of each. Moisten the edge of the paste with cold water, fold over in a half-moon shape, and coat carefully with egg and breadcrumbs, or, if preferred, egg and crushed vermicelli. Have ready a deep pan of hot fat, fry the rissoles to a golden-brown colour, then drain well, dish up and serve.

This should be sufficient for about 10 rissoles.

LOBSTER SALAD. (Salade de Homard.)

Have ready 1 hen lobster, lettuces, endive, small salad (whatever is in season), a little chopped beetroot, 2 hard-boiled eggs, a few slices of cucumber. For dressing: 4 tablespoonfuls of oil, 2 tablespoonfuls of vinegar, 1 teaspoonful of made mustard, the yolks of 2 eggs, cayenne and salt to taste, a few drops of anchovy-essence. These ingredients should be mixed perfectly smooth, and form a creamy sauce.

Wash the salad, and thoroughly dry it by shaking it in a cloth. Tear up the lettuces and endive, pour the dressing on them, and lightly mix in the small salad. Blend all well together with the meat of the lobster. Pick the meat from the claws, cut it up into nice square pieces, put half in the salad, and reserve the other half for garnishing. Separate the yolks from the whites of 2 hard-boiled eggs, chop the whites finely, and rub the yokes through a sieve. Arrange the salad lightly on a glass dish, and garnish, first with a row of sliced cucumber, then with the pieces of lobster, the yolks and whites of the eggs, coral and beetroot placed alternately, and arrange in small separate groups, so that the colours contrast nicely. Tinned lobsters may be used.

Note.—A few crayfish make an effective garnish to lobster salad.

CHEESE AND EGG DISHES

1. Cheese Straws.   2. Scotch Eggs.   3. Cheese Tartlets.

SAVOURIES

LOBSTER, SCALLOPED. (Escaloppes de Homard.)

Take 1 hen lobster, ¼ of a pint of white sauce, 2 yolks of eggs, ½ a teaspoonful of anchovy-essence, butter, breadcrumbs, cayenne, salt and pepper.

Remove the spawn, pound it with 1 oz. of butter, and pass it through a fine sieve. Cut the flesh of the lobster into small dice. Heat the sauce, add the pounded spawn, ½ a teaspoonful of anchovy-essence, cayenne and seasoning to taste. Stir over the fire for a few minutes, add the lobster and yolks of eggs, and continue to stir and cook slowly for 2 or 3 minutes longer. Turn into well-buttered scallop shells, or the lobster shell if preferred, and add a thin layer of breadcrumbs. Sprinkle lightly with salt and pepper, add a few small pieces of butter, and bake in a moderate oven for about ½ an hour. Serve as hot as possible.

This should be sufficient for 4 or 5 persons.

MACARONI AU GRATIN.

With 4 oz. of macaroni and 4 oz. of grated cheese prepare 1 pint of White sauce (p. 124) and procure a small piece of butter, some brown breadcrumbs, salt and pepper.

Break the macaroni into pieces about 1½ inches long, put them into rapidly-boiling salted water and boil for about 20 minutes, or until the macaroni is tender. If not required for immediate use, cover the macaroni with cold water to prevent the pieces sticking together. Cover the bottom of a well-buttered baking-dish with white sauce, sprinkle liberally with cheese, seasoning to taste, and add a layer of macaroni. Repeat these processes; cover the last layer of macaroni thickly with sauce, sprinkle the entire surface lightly with brown breadcrumbs, and add a few small pieces of butter. Bake in a quick oven for about 20 minutes, then serve in the dish in which it is cooked.

This should be sufficient for 6 or 7 persons.

MARROW TOAST. (Croûtes à la Moëlle.)

Make some pieces of buttered toast and take the marrow from 2 beef bones and a little salt and pepper.

Soak the marrow in tepid water for about 2 hours. About 15 minutes before the dish is wanted cut the marrow into inch lengths, place them in cold water, bring rapidly to boiling-point, and drain well. Have some squares of very hot, well-buttered toast, put the marrow on them, breaking it up and spreading it with a fork, and season with salt and pepper. Place the toast before the fire or in a hot oven until the marrow is thoroughly melted, then serve as hot as possible. When savoury marrow is preferred, sprinkle the above with chopped parsley, chives, and lemon-juice, just before serving.

This should be sufficient for 6 or 7 persons.

MARROW WITH MAÎTRE D'HÔTEL SAUCE.
(Moëlle à la Maître d'Hôtel.)

Have ready the marrow from 2 beef bones and some pieces of buttered toast. For the sauce take 2 tablespoonfuls of good White sauce (*see* **Sauces**), 1 tablespoonful of cream or milk, 1 teaspoonful of finely-chopped parsley, a few drops of lemon-juice and some Krona pepper.

Put the sauce and cream or milk into a small stewpan, and when hot add lemon-juice and seasoning to taste. Prepare the marrow toast as in the preceding recipe, pour the sauce over, and serve as quickly as possible.

This should be sufficient for 6 or 7 persons.

MEAT TOAST SAVOURY.

Take 2 tablespoonfuls of finely-chopped cold meat of any description, 2 tablespoonfuls of gravy or milk, 1 egg, 2 rounds of buttered toast, ½ an oz. of butter, salt and pepper.

Warm the butter and meat in a stewpan, beat the egg slightly, add the gravy or milk, season to taste, pour the mixture into the stewpan, and stir until the egg begins to set. Have the toast ready, trim the edges and cut into finger shapes, spread on the preparation, and serve. The above may be varied by the addition of parsley, onion, herbs or ketchup, Worcester sauce, etc.

This should be sufficient for 2 or 3 persons.

MINCE CROUSTADES SAVOURY.

With 3 pork sausages take 2 slices of streaky bacon, 6 coarsely-chopped button mushrooms, 3 tablespoonfuls of Brown or Tomato sauce (*see* **Sauces**), ½ a teaspoonful of finely-chopped parsley, milk, 1 egg, breadcrumbs, frying-fat, salt and pepper and a few sprigs of crisply fried parsley.

Place the bacon in a hot frying-pan, and fry until rather

crisp; prick the sausages, and fry them in the bacon fat. When cool, cut both into small dice, first removing the skins of the sausages, put them with the sauce, mushrooms and parsley into a stewpan, season to taste, and re-heat. To make the croustades, cut 1-inch slices from a stale loaf, stamp out 6 round or oval shapes, and scoop out the inside, forming a hollow to hold the mince. Now dip them in milk, let them become moistened without being sodden, then coat them with egg and breadcrumbs, and fry in hot fat until nicely browned. Have the mince ready, fill the cases, garnish with fried parsley, and serve.

This should be sufficient for 6 persons.

MUSHROOMS AU GRATIN. (Champignons au gratin.)

Procure some fresh mushrooms and have ready grated Parmesan cheese, breadcrumbs, finely-chopped parsley, chopped shallot, butter, salt and pepper.

Wash and peel the mushrooms, place them in a fireproof baking-dish, sprinkle them lightly with salt, pepper, shallot, parsley and cheese, and thickly with breadcrumbs, add a few small pieces of butter, bake in a moderately hot oven for about 15 minutes, then serve in the dish.

Allow ½ a lb. of mushrooms for 6 or 7 persons.

MUSHROOMS, GRILLED. (Champignons grillés.)

With some cup mushrooms take some pepper and salt, butter and lemon-juice.

Carefully peel the mushrooms, cut off a portion of the stalk, and season with salt. Grill them over a clear fire, turning them once, and arrange them on a very hot dish. Put a small piece of butter on each mushroom, season to taste with pepper and salt, and squeeze over them a few drops of lemon-juice.

Allow 2 mushrooms to each person and 1 or 2 over.

MUSHROOMS ON TOAST. (Champignons sur Croûtes.)

Have ready an equal number of medium-sized mushrooms and slightly larger rounds of well-buttered toast and some butter, salt and pepper.

Peel the mushrooms, cut off a portion of the stalks, season well with salt and pepper, brush over with warm butter, and grill over a clear fire, or fry in a pan in a little hot butter. Arrange neatly on the hot-buttered toast croûtes, and serve as hot as possible.

Allow 2 mushrooms to each person and 1 or 2 over.

MUSHROOM SOUFFLÉ.

To 6 large mushrooms peeled and finely chopped allow 1 oz. of butter, 1 oz. of flour, 3 yolks of eggs, 4 whites of eggs, $\frac{1}{4}$ of a pint of milk, salt and pepper.

Melt the butter, stir in the flour, add the milk, and boil gently for a few minutes, stirring briskly meanwhile. Beat each yolk of egg in separately, stir in the minced mushrooms, and season to taste. Whisk the whites of eggs stiffly, stir them lightly into the mixture, and turn the whole into a well-buttered soufflé-tin or case. Bake in a fairly hot oven for about $\frac{1}{2}$ an hour, and serve at once.

This should be sufficient for 4 or 5 persons.

MUSHROOMS, STUFFED. (Champignons farcis au gratin.)

Have ready 6 medium-sized mushrooms, 6 round croûtes of fried or toasted bread, slightly larger than the mushrooms, 1 tablespoonful of finely-chopped cooked ham, $\frac{1}{2}$ a tablespoonful of breadcrumbs, a teaspoonful of grated Parmesan cheese, 1 teaspoonful of finely-chopped mushrooms, $\frac{1}{2}$ a teaspoonful of finely-chopped parsley, 1 very small onion finely-chopped, $\frac{1}{2}$ an oz. of butter, salt and pepper, browned breadcrumbs and some Brown sauce (p. 121).

Remove the stalks and skins, trim the mushrooms to a uniform shape with a round cutter, and use the trimmings for the mixture. Melt $\frac{1}{3}$ of an oz. of butter in a small stewpan, add to it all the above ingredients, except the brown breadcrumbs and brown sauce, season well with salt and pepper, stir briskly over the fire until well mixed, adding by degrees as much brown sauce as is necessary slightly to moisten the whole. Pile the preparation on the mushrooms, sprinkle with browned breadcrumbs, add a small piece of butter, and bake from 10 to 15 minutes in a moderate oven. Serve as hot as possible.

This should be sufficient for 5 or 6 persons.

SAVOURIES

OMELET PLAIN. (Omelette Naturel.)

Take 4 eggs, 2 tablespoonfuls of cream or milk, $1\frac{1}{2}$ oz. of butter, salt and pepper.

Beat the eggs just long enough to mix the yolks and whites well together, and add the cream and seasoning. Melt the butter in an omelet-pan, and remove the scum as it rises. Pour in the mixture, stir with a fork until the eggs begin to set, then fold the sides towards the middle in an oblong form ; or draw the mixture towards the handle of the pan, thus forming a half-moon shape. Turn over on to a hot dish, and serve quickly.

This should be sufficient for 2 or 3 persons.

Note.—Minced cooked ham, tongue, chicken, meat or fish may be mixed with the eggs, or if raw, fried in the butter before putting in the eggs. Such additions as sliced tomatoes, kidneys, etc., are folded inside the omelet when it is partially or completely cooked.

OMELET WITH HERBS. (Omelette aux Fines Herbes.)

Have ready 4 eggs, 3 tablespoonfuls of cream or milk, $\frac{1}{2}$ a teaspoonful of finely-chopped parsley, $\frac{1}{8}$ of a teaspoonful of finely-chopped shallot or onion, a pinch of mixed herbs, salt and pepper and $1\frac{1}{2}$ oz. of butter.

Beat the eggs until light, add the cream or milk, parsley, shallot and herbs, and season with salt and pepper. Melt the butter in an omelet-pan, pour in the mixture, stir with a fork until the eggs are on the point of setting, then, with a spoon, draw it quickly towards the handle of the pan in the shape of a crescent. Turn over on to a hot dish, and serve.

This should be sufficient for 2 or 3 persons.

OYSTER FRITTERS. (Beignets aux Huîtres.)

Take 12 large oysters, 3 oz. of flour, $\frac{1}{4}$ of a pint of tepid water, 1 tablespoonful of salad-oil or oiled butter, the whites of 2 eggs, salt and some frying-fat.

Make a batter by stirring the water and salad-oil gradually into the flour ; when perfectly smooth add the salt, and lastly the stiffly-whisked whites of eggs. Beard the oysters, dip them in the batter, and fry them in hot fat until they acquire a golden-brown colour.

This should be sufficient for 6 persons.

Note.—Oysters are in season from September to April.

OYSTER FRITTERS. (Another Method.)

Have ready 12 oysters, 12 small thin slices of bacon, ½ a lemon, parsley, frying-fat, and frying-batter.

Sprinkle the oysters with lemon-juice, and roll each one in a slice of bacon just large enough to enclose it. Make the batter as directed in preceding recipe, put in the prepared oysters 1 or 2 at a time, take them out on the point of a skewer, drain slightly, and at once drop them into hot fat. Fry a pale golden-brown colour, drain well, and serve garnished with crisply-fried parsley.

This should be sufficient for 6 persons.

OYSTER SAUSAGES.

With 12 sauce oysters take 1 lb. of veal, ¼ of a lb. of suet finely chopped, ¼ of a lb. of stale bread, 1 egg, butter or dripping for frying, salt and pepper.

Open the oysters, preserve the liquor, remove the beards and cut the oysters into very small pieces. Strain the liquor over the bread, let it soak until soft, then drain off any unabsorbed liquor, and beat the bread with a fork until no lumps remain. Pass the veal 2 or 3 times through a mincing-machine, add the suet, bread, salt and pepper to taste, and lastly the oysters and egg. The preparation may be improved by being well pounded in a mortar, but it is not absolutely necessary. When ready, press into skins, or shape in the form of small sausages, roll lightly in flour seasoned with salt and pepper, and fry in hot butter or fat.

This should be sufficient for about 8 small sausages.

OYSTERS, FRIED. (Fritot d'Huîtres.)

Take 8 or 10 oysters, some fat bacon, 8 or 10 round croûtes of fried bread, ½ a teaspoonful of very finely-chopped shallot, ½ a teaspoonful of finely-chopped parsley, lemon-juice, Krona pepper, frying-fat, and some frying batter. (*See* **Oyster Fritters,** p. 53.)

Beard the oysters, slice the bacon very thinly, and with a sharp cutter stamp out small rounds from 1½ to 1¾ inches in diameter. Season the oysters with lemon-juice and Krona pepper, place each one between 2 rounds of bacon, pressing the edges firmly together. Make the batter as directed, season it well with Krona pepper, add the shallot and parsley, then dip in the rounds and fry them in hot fat until nicely browned and crisp. Drain well, and serve on the prepared croûtes of fried bread, sprinkled with some finely-chopped parsley or Krona pepper.

This should be sufficient for 6 or 7 persons.

Note.—Oysters are in season from September to April.

OYSTERS IN CASES. (Huîtres en Caisses à la Diable.)

With 12 large oysters take 2 or 3 tablespoonfuls of White sauce (p. 124), 1 tablespoonful of grated Parmesan cheese, butter, breadcrumbs, cayenne and 8 or 9 china or paper soufflé-cases.

Beard the oysters, cut each one into 4 pieces, strain the liquor into the white sauce, and boil until slightly reduced. Let the sauce cool, then add it to the oysters, half the cheese, and cayenne to taste. Brush the soufflé-cases over with oiled butter, and fill them with the preparation. Mix the remainder of the cheese with an equal quantity of bread-crumbs, cover the surface of the ragoût lightly with this mixture, add a few drops of oiled butter, and bake for 5 or 6 minutes in a hot oven.

This should be sufficient for 8 or 9 persons.

OYSTERS IN SHELLS. (Huîtres Gratinées en Coquilles.)

To 18 oysters allow 3 tablespoonfuls of Béchamel sauce (p. 121), 1 oz. of butter, ½ a lemon, a few grains of cayenne, ½ cupful of white breadcrumbs, and a few sprigs of parsley for garnish.

Open the oysters, remove the beards, strain and preserve the liquor. Wash 9 deep shells, dry them, and coat the insides with butter. Put a teaspoonful of Béchamel sauce in each shell, also a few drops of liquor and lemon-juice, lay the oysters on the top, season with a little cayenne, and cover with sauce. Sprinkle the entire surface with breadcrumbs, lay a small piece of butter on the top of each, and brown them slightly in a hot oven.

This should be sufficient for 9 coquilles.

OYSTERS ON TOAST. (Huîtres sur Canapés.)

Have ready 12 oysters, cooked ham, thin slices of white or brown bread, butter, salt, cayenne and a few sprigs of crisply fried parsley.

Toast some thin slices of either white or brown bread, and from them cut 12 rounds from 1½ to 2 inches in diameter. Cover each one with a round of ham of corresponding size and place on it an oyster, previously bearded. Season with a little salt and a tiny pinch of cayenne, add a small piece of butter, then bake in a hot oven for about 3 minutes. Dish on a folded napkin or dish-paper, garnish with fried parsley, and serve.

This should be sufficient for 12 canapés.

OYSTERS, SCALLOPED. (Escaloppes aux Huîtres.)

Take 12 large or 18 small oysters, 2 or 3 tablespoonfuls of thick white sauce, some lemon-juice, white breadcrumbs, butter, pepper and salt.

Blanch the oysters in their own liquor, remove the beards, and cut them in halves. Strain the liquor into the white sauce, boil until sufficiently reduced, then add lemon-juice, salt and pepper to taste. Brush 8 or 9 small scallop shells over with nearly cold clarified butter, and coat them with the breadcrumbs. Distribute the oysters equally, add the prepared sauce, cover lightly with breadcrumbs, put 2 or 3 morsels of butter on the top of each and bake in a quick oven until nicely browned. Send to table, and serve as hot as possible.

This should be sufficient for 7 or 8 persons.

OYSTER TIT-BITS. (Bonnes Bouches aux Huîtres.)

Have ready 8 or 9 oysters, 8 or 9 round croûtes of 2 inches in diameter fried bread, bacon, anchovy paste, lemon-juice, butter and Krona pepper.

Beard the oysters, place them between 2 plates with their own liquor and a small piece of butter, and warm in the oven or over a saucepan of boiling water. Spread each croûte with anchovy paste, cover with a stamped-out round of very thin fried bacon, and place an oyster on the top of each. Sprinkle with lemon-juice and Krona pepper, and serve as hot as possible.

This should be sufficient for 6 or 7 persons.

ROES ON TOAST. (*See* Cod's Roe Croûtes, p. 36; Herring Roe Croûtes, p. 42; and Herring Roe Tit-Bits, p. 42.)

SAVOURIES

SALMON DARIOLES À LA MOSCOVIENNE.

With about 1 lb. of cooked salmon take 6 large oysters, 1 large truffle, 1 hard-boiled egg, ½ an oz. of anchovy paste, a teaspoonful of tarragon vinegar, ¼ of a gill of cream, about ½ a pint of aspic jelly, 4 filleted anchovies, a few slices of cucumber, red chillies, a pinch of cayenne, salt and pepper and a little grated nutmeg.

Flake the salmon, line 8 or 9 small dariole, bouchée, or timbale moulds with a thin layer of aspic jelly, decorate with a few thin slices of truffle, some nice flakes of salmon, and a few strips of red chillies. Set the garnish well with a little aspic, and put it aside to cool. Pound the remainder of the fish in a mortar together with 6 cooked oysters, the hard-boiled egg, and the anchovy paste; season with a pinch of cayenne pepper, salt, and a little grated nutmeg. Rub through a fine sieve, add the tarragon vinegar, the cream, and about 1 gill of aspic jelly, mix the ingredients well together and then fill the moulds. Put the anchovy fillets and a few slices of truffles between the farce, or stuffing, in filling. If the mixture does not quite fill the moulds, supply the deficiency with aspic jelly, and stand the moulds on the ice until required. For serving, immerse the moulds in tepid water, turn out the contents quickly, and place them on a round dish, garnish round the sides with chopped aspic and a few fancifully-cut slices of cucumber.

This should be sufficient for 7 or 8 persons.

SALMON, SMOKED, DEVILLED.

Procure about ½ a lb. of smoked salmon and have ready 3 to 4 slices of toasted bread, 1 oz. of fresh butter, curry butter (p. 103), cayenne, salt and pepper.

Trim the slices of toast and cut each into 3 even-sized pieces, and butter one side of each, next sprinkle with salt, pepper and cayenne, then cover them with thin slices of smoked salmon, and add a layer of devilled butter. Place them in a hot oven for a few minutes. Dish up neatly, garnish with sprigs of parsley and serve nice and hot.

This should be sufficient for 7 or 8 persons.

SARDINE CANAPÉS. (*See* **Sardine Croustades**, p. 58; **Sardines with Tomatoes**, p. 61; **Sardines with Capers**, p. 60.)

SARDINE CROUSTADES. (Croustades de Sardines.)

With 2 large or 3 small sardines take 1 tablespoonful of White or Tomato sauce (*see* **Sauces**), 1 teaspoonful of grated Parmesan cheese, a few drops of lemon-juice, a few grains of cayenne pepper, stale bread, clarified butter or fat and watercress.

Cut slices of stale bread from ½ to ¾ of an inch in thickness, stamp out 8 or 9 rounds or oval shapes about 2 inches in diameter, and with a smaller cutter make an inner circle or oval ⅓ of an inch from the outer edge of the croustade. Fry them in hot clarified butter or fat until lightly browned, then with the point of a small sharp knife lift out the inner ring, remove all moist crumb, place them in a moderate oven to become crisp and dry, and cool before using. Meanwhile skin and bone the sardines, divide them into fine ½-inch strips, put them with the sauce into a small stewpan, and, when using white sauce, add also a few drops of anchovy-essence. Season to taste with salt and cayenne, add a few drops of lemon-juice, and when thoroughly hot stir in the cheese. Fill the croustades with the preparation, garnish with watercress seasoned with oil and vinegar. Send to table, and serve as quickly as possible.

This should be sufficient for 7 or 8 persons.

SARDINE ECLAIRS. (Eclairs de Sardines.) (*See* **Anchovy Eclairs**, p. 30.)

SARDINE PATTIES. (Bouchées de Sardines.)

Take 2 large or 3 small sardines, 1 tablespoonful of White sauce (*see* **Sauces**), 1 teaspoonful of grated Parmesan cheese, a few drops of lemon-juice, a few drops of anchovy-essence, cayenne, some Puff-paste and fried parsley.

Prepare 8 patty-cases 1½ inches in diameter (*see* **Caviare Patties**, p. 33), when baked, remove and put aside the lids, scoop out the soft inside, and keep the cases hot until required. Skin and bone the sardines, and divide them into fine ½-inch strips. Put the sauce and sardines into a small stewpan; when hot, add the anchovy-essence, lemon-juice and cayenne to taste, and stir in the cheese. Fill the cases with the preparation, put on the lids, garnish with crisply-fried parsley, and serve.

This should be sufficient for 6 or 7 persons.

SARDINE TOAST. (Croûtes de Sardines.)

Have ready 4 sardines, ½ an oz. of butter, 1 egg, 2 tablespoonfuls of milk, 1 teaspoonful of essence of anchovy, 2 or 3 pieces of toast, butter and cayenne.

Skin and bone the sardines and chop them coarsely. Put the milk and butter into a stewpan; when hot, add the prepared sardines, anchovy-essence and a little cayenne, and last of all the yolk of the egg. Stir by the side of the fire until the egg thickens, but do not let it boil, or it may curdle. Have ready well-buttered squares of toast, pour on the preparation, and serve as quickly as possible.

This should be sufficient for 3 or 4 persons.

SARDINES, DEVILLED. (Sardines à la Diable.)

To 8 or 10 sardines allow 8 or 10 fried finger-shaped croûtes, 1 oz. of butter, 1 finely-chopped shallot, lemon-juice, cayenne, Krona pepper and salt.

Skin the sardines, split them down the back, remove the bone, and replace the 2 halves. Sprinkle them with lemon-juice, shallot, cayenne, and salt, cover and let them remain for half an hour, during which time they must be turned once, and again sprinkled with lemon-juice, etc. Heat the butter in a sauté-pan, drain and dry the sardines, rub them over lightly with flour, and fry them until nicely browned. Meanwhile fry the croûtes in clarified butter or fat, lay on each a sardine, sprinkle with lemon-juice and Krona pepper, and serve.

This should be sufficient for 6 or 8 persons.

SARDINES, FRIED. (Beignets de Sardines.)

With 4 or 5 sardines take ½ a teaspoonful of finely-chopped parsley, 1 finely-chopped shallot, 1 teaspoonful of lemon-juice, cayenne, Krona pepper, frying-fat and frying-batter (*see* **Oyster Fritters**, p. 53).

Skin, bone and divide the sardines in halves, sprinkle over them the lemon-juice, parsley and shallot, cover with a plate, and let them remain for 1 hour. Make the batter as directed, dip in the sardines, fry them in hot fat until nicely browned, then drain well. Arrange in a pyramidal form on a hot dish, sprinkle with Krona pepper, and serve.

This should be sufficient for 6 or 8 persons.

Note.—For another method of frying, *see* **Anchovy Aigrettes.** Four sardines may be substituted for the anchovies.

SARDINES, GRILLED. (*See* **Sardines, Devilled,** p. 59.)

Prepare the sardines as directed, but instead of frying them, grill them over, or in front of, a clear fire.

SARDINES WITH CAPERS. (Sardines aux Câpres.)

Take 4 or 5 sardines, 1 level dessertspoonful of finely-chopped capers, 2 tablespoonfuls of liquid meat-glaze, grated Parmesan cheese, buttered toast or fried finger-shaped croûtons and a little cayenne.

Skin and bone the sardines, and divide them in halves. Prepare the croûtes or cut the toast into fingers, place half a sardine on each, add a few grains of cayenne, sprinkle liberally with cheese, cover with a buttered paper, and make thoroughly hot in the oven. Heat the glaze, add to it the capers, pour it over the sardines, and serve hot.

This should be sufficient for 6 or 8 persons.

SARDINES WITH MAÎTRE D'HÔTEL SAUCE. (Sardines à la Maître d'Hôtel.)

Have ready 4 or 5 sardines, 2 tablespoonfuls of thick White sauce (p. 124), 1 teaspoonful of finely-chopped parsley, 1 teaspoonful of lemon-juice, toast, butter and Krona pepper.

Skin and bone the sardines, and divide them in halves. Cut the toast into fingers, butter them well, place half a sardine on each, season with Krona pepper, cover with a buttered paper, and make thoroughly hot in the oven. Meanwhile, add the parsley and lemon-juice to the hot white sauce, season to taste, and when ready to serve pour it over the sardines and toast.

This should be sufficient for 6 or 8 persons.

SARDINES WITH PARMESAN. (Sardines au-Parmesan.)

Procure some sardines, 2 oz. of grated Parmesan cheese, 4 oz. of flour, 1 oz. of oiled butter, 1 egg, salt and pepper, cayenne, frying-fat, Krona pepper.

Mix the flour, a dessertspoonful of cheese, a saltspoonful of salt, and a good pinch of cayenne together, add the yolk of the egg and as much cold water as is needed to form a stiff paste. Knead well for at least 10 minutes, then put the paste aside in a cool place for at least 1 hour. Meanwhile remove the skin and tails from the sardines, take out the backbone and replace the two halves, then dip each sardine in oiled butter and coat lightly with cheese. Roll the paste out as thinly as possible, and cut it into oblong strips just large enough to enclose a sardine. Moisten the edges of the paste with white of egg, place the sardines on one half, fold the other over, and pinch the edges together. Drop them into hot fat, fry until golden-brown, then drain well, sprinkle with grated cheese and Krona pepper, and serve.

SARDINES WITH TOMATOES. (Sardines à la Napolitaine.)

With 8 small or 4 large sardines take 8 finger-shaped croûtes of fried bread or buttered toast, 2 tomatoes, 1 teaspoonful of cornflour, 1 teaspoonful of grated Parmesan cheese, pepper and salt.

Skin the sardines, remove the bones, and divide them in halves if large. Squeeze as much juice as possible from the tomatoes, and rub the pulp through a fine sieve. Put it into a small stewpan; when hot add the cornflour, previously blended with a little tomato-juice, and stir until it thickens. Season with salt and pepper, stir in the cheese, and spread each croûte lightly with the preparation. Lay the sardines on the top, cover with a thin layer of the tomato mixture, place in the oven until thoroughly hot, then serve.

This should be sufficient for 6 or 8 persons.

SCALLOPS AND MUSHROOMS. (Pétoncles aux Champignons.)

Take 6 scallops, 6 large flat mushrooms, 1 oz. of butter, 1 or 2 tablespoonfuls of white sauce, milk, salt and pepper.

Remove the scallops from their shells, and wash well in cold water. Put them into a stewpan with just sufficient milk to cover, add a little salt and pepper and simmer gently for about 50 minutes. Drain well, chop the yellow and white parts separately, moisten with a little white sauce, and season to taste. While the scallops are cooking remove the stalks of the mushrooms, peel them and fry them in hot butter. Place an equal portion of the white part of the scallops on each mushroom, pile the red part on the top, make thoroughly hot in the oven, and serve.

This should be sufficient for 5 or 6 persons.

SCALLOPS, FRIED. (Pétoncles frits.)

Procure 12 scallops, 1 egg, ½ an oz. of butter, 2 oz. of flour, 1 gill of milk, salt, pepper and cayenne, frying-fat and a few sprigs of parsley.

Drain the scallops on a cloth. Prepare the batter as follows: Sift the flour into a basin, add a pinch of salt. Melt the butter, beat up the egg, stir both into the flour, add the milk, and work until quite smooth. If too thick, a little more melted butter or milk may be added. Let the batter stand for an hour, then stir in a dessertspoonful of chopped parsley. Season the scallops with a little salt, a good pinch of white pepper, and a small pinch of cayenne. Dip them into the batter, drop them one by one into hot fat, fry from 5 to 6 minutes to a golden-brown, drain on a cloth, pile up on a hot dish, garnish with fried parsley, and serve with lobster or Tomato sauce (p. 124).

This should be sufficient for about 8 or 9 persons.

Note.—Scallops are in season from October to April.

SCALLOPS IN SHELLS.

With 12 scallops take a cupful of breadcrumbs, 1 oz. of butter, 1 gill of white sauce, cayenne, and salt, a little chopped parsley, and a squeeze of lemon.

Trim the scallops by cutting off the beards and black parts, cleanse 6 shells, butter them, and strew in a few breadcrumbs. Put scallops in each, season them with the cayenne and chopped parsley, and a drop or two of lemon-juice. Put a little pepper and salt with the breadcrumbs, cover the scallops with white sauce, sprinkle with breadcrumbs, place little pieces of butter on the top, and bake for about 20 minutes.

This should be sufficient for 6 persons.

SCALLOPS, SCALLOPED.

Take 12 scallops, 1 teaspoonful of finely-chopped parsley, some breadcrumbs, White sauce (p. 124), butter, and a little salt and pepper.

Wash and drain the scallops, chop them finely, and mix with them an equal quantity of breadcrumbs and sufficient white sauce to bind. Season to taste with salt and pepper, and add the parsley. Wash and dry the deeper shells, butter them thickly, and sprinkle lightly with breadcrumbs. Fill the shells with the preparation, cover the surface lightly with breadcrumbs, and add 2 or 3 bits of butter. Bake in a moderate oven until well-browned, and serve in the shells.

This should be sufficient for 8 or 9 persons.

SCALLOPS, STEWED.

Procure 12 scallops, 1 oz. of butter, 1 oz. of flour, lemon-juice or vinegar, salt and pepper.

Open the shells like an oyster, remove the scallops, and trim away the beard and black parts. Wash well in 2 or 3 waters, then cover them with warm water, and boil gently from 50 to 60 minutes. Meanwhile knead the flour and butter well together, mix in a little salt and pepper, separate into small pieces, and add them to the contents of the stewpan 20 minutes before serving. When ready, place the scallops on a hot dish, season the sauce to taste, add the lemon-juice or vinegar, and pour over the fish.

This should be sufficient for 8 or 9 persons.

SCOTCH WOODCOCK. (Anchois à l'Ecossaise.)

Have ready the yolks of 2 eggs, 1 gill of cream (or cream and milk in equal parts), anchovy paste, some pieces of hot toast, butter, cayenne and salt.

Cut the toast into 2-inch squares, butter well, and spread them with anchovy paste. Season the yolks with a little cayenne and salt; when slightly beaten add them to the hot cream, stir over the fire until they thicken sufficiently, then pour the preparation over the toast, and serve as hot as possible.

This should be sufficient for 6 or 8 persons.

SCRAMBLED EGGS. (*See* Recipe, p. 91.)

SHRIMP MOULDS. (Petits Pains de Crevettes.)

With ½ a pint of picked shrimps take 1 gill of cream or milk, 1 gill of stock, 2 eggs, 3 Spanish olives, 2 finely-chopped gherkins, 1 tablespoonful of chutney, red panurette breadcrumbs, cayenne and a little salt.

Stone the olives, pound them well with the shrimps, gherkins and chutney in a mortar until smooth, adding the eggs separately and the stock gradually, then pass through a fine sieve. Season with cayenne and salt, then add the cream, previously stiffly whipped, or milk. Have ready 8 well-buttered timbale or dariole moulds, sprinkle them with red panurette breadcrumbs (this useful preparation is sold in packets), and turn the mixture into them. Place the moulds in a sauté-pan, surround them with boiling water, and steam gently for about 20 minutes. Serve with watercress sauce.

This should be sufficient for 6 or 7 persons.

SHRIMP TOAST. (Crevettes sur Croûtes.)

To $\frac{1}{4}$ of a pint of picked shrimps allow a little anchovy paste, $\frac{1}{2}$ an oz. of butter, 1 egg, 1 tablespoonful of milk, salt and cayenne and prepare 8 croûtes of buttered toast.

Melt the butter in a stewpan, put in the shrimps, and when hot add the eggs and milk previously beaten together, salt and cayenne to taste, and stir by the side of the fire until the mixture thickens. Meanwhile spread the toast lightly with anchovy paste, and now add the shrimp preparation, and serve as hot as possible.

This should be sufficient for 6 or 7 persons.

SHRIMPS, CURRIED. (Crevettes au Kari.)

Procure $\frac{1}{4}$ of a pint of shelled shrimps and take 1 oz. of butter, 1 finely-chopped shallot, $\frac{1}{2}$ a gill of cream, $\frac{1}{2}$ a gill of stock, 1 teaspoonful of curry-powder and $\frac{1}{2}$ a teaspoonful of lemon-juice.

Cut the shrimps across in halves. Fry the shallot slightly in butter, add the curry-powder, and cook it for 3 minutes, then pour in the stock and stir until it boils. Let it simmer very gently for 15 minutes, put in the shrimps, cream, lemon-juice, and add the necessary seasoning. Make thoroughly hot, and serve in china ramakin-cases.

This should be sufficient for 5 or 6 persons.

SMOKED HADDOCK CROUSTADES. (Croustades à la St. George.)

Take $\frac{1}{2}$ a small dried haddock, 1 oz. of butter, $\frac{1}{2}$ a pint of milk, 2 eggs, 1 finely-chopped shallot, 1 teaspoonful of finely-chopped parsley, brown bread, nutmeg, pepper and Krona pepper.

Pour boiling water over the fish, and let it remain covered for 10 minutes, then remove the skin and bones, and divide

DRESSED VEGETABLES

1. Wafer Potatoes. 2. Mushroom Soufflés. 3. Stuffed Tomatoes.

the haddock into large flakes. Place these in a stewpan with the hot milk, simmer gently for 10 minutes, then strain, put the milk aside, and chop the fish finely. Heat the butter in a stewpan, fry the shallot without browning, then put in the fish and parsley, and when hot add the eggs previously beaten with 2 tablespoonfuls of the milk in which the haddock was cooked. Season to taste with pepper and nutmeg, and stir by the side of the fire until the mixture thickens. Meanwhile prepare 8 croustades of brown bread (*see* **Sardine Croustades**, p. 58), fill them with the fish preparation, garnish with parsley and Krona pepper, and serve as hot as possible.

This should be sufficient for 6 or 7 persons.

SMOKED HADDOCK CROÛTES. (Croûtes de Merluche fumée.)

Have ready 2 tablespoonfuls of finely-chopped cooked haddock, $\frac{1}{2}$ an oz. of butter, $\frac{1}{2}$ an oz. of flour, $\frac{1}{4}$ of a pint of milk, anchovy-essence, $\frac{1}{2}$ a teaspoonful of finely-chopped parsley, Krona pepper, cayenne, 8 round croûtes (2 inches in diameter) of fried bread.

Prepare the fried bread croûtes as in previous recipe. Heat the butter in a small stewpan, stir in the flour, pour in the milk, and boil well. Add the fish, anchovy-essence, Krona pepper, and cayenne to taste, and stir until thoroughly hot. Pile lightly on the croûtes, garnish with parsley and Krona pepper, and serve as hot as possible.

This should be sufficient for 6 or 7 persons.

SMOKED HADDOCK, FILLETED. (Filets de Merluche fumée.)

To 1 medium-sized smoked haddock, or $\frac{1}{2}$ a large one (preferably the latter), allow 2 oz. of butter, 1 teaspoonful of finely-chopped parsley, pepper and a little lemon-juice.

Cook the haddock for 10 minutes in the oven in a tin containing a little water, remove the skin and bones, and divide the fish into fillets of a convenient size for serving. Have the butter ready melted in a baking-dish, put in the fish and the parsley, season with pepper, baste well with butter, and cook for 10 minutes in the oven, repeating the basting at short intervals. Place the fish carefully on a hot dish, add a little lemon-juice to the sauce, pour it over the fish, and serve.

This should be sufficient for 4 or 5 persons.

SMOKED HADDOCK SOUFFLÉ. (Soufflé de Merluche fumée.)

With 1 small cooked smoked haddock take 1 oz. of butter, 2 eggs, anchovy-essence, cayenne, Krona pepper, 8 or 9 china or paper soufflé-cases and a little clarified butter.

Coat the soufflé-cases thickly with butter. Pound the fish whilst warm, adding the yolks of the eggs one at a time and the butter gradually, season highly with cayenne and Krona pepper, and when perfectly smooth pass through a fine sieve. Whisk the whites of egg to a stiff froth, stir them lightly into the mixture, fill the cases three parts full, and bake in a quick oven for about 10 minutes. Sprinkle with Krona pepper, and serve quickly.

This should be sufficient for 6 or 7 persons.

SPRATS FRIED IN BATTER. (Melettes frites.)

Procure $\frac{1}{2}$ a lb. of sprats, 1 teaspoonful of finely-chopped parsley, $\frac{1}{4}$ of a teaspoonful of finely-chopped shallot or onion, $\frac{1}{4}$ of a teaspoonful of powdered mixed herbs, $\frac{1}{4}$ of a teaspoonful of grated lemon-rind, Frying-batter (*see* **Oyster Fritters**, p. 53), salad-oil or clarified fat, parsley, salt and pepper.

Wipe or wash the fish, and if liked, cut off the heads and tails, but do not open them. Make the batter as directed, add to it the parsley, shallot, herbs, lemon-rind, and a good seasoning of pepper, dip in the sprats, taking care to coat them completely, and fry them in hot oil or fat in a frying-pan until nicely browned. Drain well, and serve garnished with fried parsley.

This should be sufficient for 4 or 5 persons.

SWEETBREAD, MOULDED WITH ASPARAGUS. (Ris de Veau aux Asperges.)

Have ready some blanched sweetbread, blanched asparagus, chicken quenelle mixture, well-reduced Béchamel sauce (p. 121) and cooked tongue.

To make the chicken quenelle mixture, melt $\frac{1}{2}$ an oz. of butter, stir in 2 oz. of flour, add $\frac{1}{4}$ of a pint of stock or water and let boil whilst stirring. Put aside to cool. Shred 8 oz. of raw chicken meat finely and pass through a mincing machine. Pound well in a mortar, adding the boiled liquor already prepared, by degrees and also 2 eggs, one at a time. Season well and rub through a fine sieve, then add 2 tablespoonfuls of cream or milk. Decorate the bottom of a buttered mould with tongue, cut in small triangular shapes, and the sides with asparagus. Mask the whole with a thick layer of quenelle mixture, fill the centre with large dice of sweetbread and shredded tongue, suitably seasoned, and moistened with Béchamel sauce, and cover with a layer of quenelle mixture. Steam very gently from 1¾ to 2 hours, unmould, dish up, and serve Béchamel sauce separately.

This should be sufficient for 6 persons.

SWISS EGGS. (Œufs à la Suisse.)

With 8 eggs take 3 tablespoonfuls of grated cheese, 1½ oz. of butter, salt and pepper and a few grains of cayenne.

Butter 8 china ramakin-cases, put a small teaspoonful of cheese at the bottom of each one, and add a little seasoning. Break the eggs carefully, keeping the yolks whole, lay 1 in each case, cover with a small teaspoonful of cheese, add a little seasoning, place a small piece of butter on the top, and bake until set. Serve hot.

This should be sufficient for 6 or 7 persons.

TOMATO SAUSAGES.

Prepare ½ a pint of tomato purée, ½ a pint of well-cooked rice, and ½ a pint of breadcrumbs, and take 1 tablespoonful of finely-chopped onion, 1 teaspoonful of powdered mixed herbs, salt and pepper.

When using fresh tomatoes, squeeze out the greater part of the juice, add it to the water in which the rice is cooked, and pass the tomato pulp through a fine sieve. Mix the rice, breadcrumbs, tomato purée, onion, herbs, and a good seasoning of salt and pepper, well together, press the mixture lightly into small-sized sausage skins, and fry in hot fat or butter until well browned.

This should be sufficient for 8 or 9 persons.

TOMATOES AND SPINACH. (Tomates aux Épinards.)

Take 8 tomatoes, 8 tablespoonfuls of spinach purée, 8 croûtes of fried bread, salt and pepper.

Remove some of the pulp and juice from the tomatoes, fill the cavities with spinach purée highly seasoned with salt and pepper, and bake in a moderately hot oven until the tomatoes are soft (about 10 minutes). Serve on the croûtes.

This should be sufficient for 6 or 7 persons.

Note.—Fresh tomatoes are in season from March to December; but they are obtainable bottled or tinned at any time.

TOMATOES, BAKED. (Tomates au gratin.)

Have ready 8 to 10 tomatoes, pepper and salt to taste, 2 oz. of butter and some breadcrumbs.

Take the stalks off the tomatoes, cut them in halves, and put them into a deep baking-dish with a seasoning of pepper, and salt and butter in the above proportion. Cover the whole with breadcrumbs; drop over these a little clarified butter, bake in a moderate oven from 20 minutes to ½ an hour, and serve very hot. The tomatoes, instead of being cut in half, may be baked whole, if preferred, but they will take rather longer to cook.

This should be sufficient for 5 or 6 persons.

TOMATOES, DEVILLED. (Tomates à la Diable.)

To 5 or 6 firm tomatoes allow 2 oz. of butter, the yolks of 2 hard-boiled eggs, 2 tablespoonfuls of vinegar, ½ a teaspoonful of made mustard, 1 saltspoonful of salt, 1 saltspoonful of sugar, a good pinch of cayenne, 2 raw eggs and a small piece of butter for frying.

Slice the tomatoes, place them in a sauté-pan containing a little hot butter, and let them cook very slowly for a few minutes. Mix the hard-boiled yolks and 2 oz. of butter together, stir in the vinegar, add the mustard, salt, sugar and cayenne, and turn the whole into a small stewpan. When thoroughly hot, beat and add the eggs, and stir until the mixture thickens. Place the tomatoes on a hot dish, pour the sauce over, and serve.

This should be sufficient for 4 or 5 persons.

TOMATOES, SCALLOPED. (Tomates en Coquille.)

Prepare ½ a pint of tomato pulp and take 2 or 3 tablespoonfuls of breadcrumbs, ½ an oz. of butter, ½ a teaspoonful of finely-chopped onion, salt and pepper, sugar, nutmeg, browned breadcrumbs and butter.

Obtain the pulp by passing tomatoes through a fine sieve, or use preserved pulp. Heat the butter in a stewpan, fry the onion until lightly browned, and add half the tomato pulp and white breadcrumbs gradually until the mixture has the consistency of very thick cream. Add a pinch each of sugar and nutmeg, season to taste with salt and pepper, and pour the mixture into well-buttered scallop shells. Cover lightly with browned breadcrumbs, add 2 or 3 small pieces of butter, bake in a moderately hot oven from 10 to 15 minutes, then serve as quickly as possible.

This should be sufficient for 6 or 8 shells.

TOMATOES, STUFFED. (Tomates farcies au gratin.)

Have ready 6 medium-sized tomatoes, 6 croûtons of fried or toasted bread, 1 heaped tablespoonful of finely-chopped lean cooked ham, ½ a tablespoonful of breadcrumbs, 1 small teaspoonful of grated cheese preferably Parmesan, 1 teaspoonful of finely-chopped mushrooms, ½ a teaspoonful of finely-chopped parsley, 1 very small onion finely chopped, ½ an oz. of butter, 1 tablespoonful of brown sauce (about), browned breadcrumbs, salt and pepper.

Remove the stalks of the tomatoes, and scoop out a little of the pulp. Mix together all the above ingredients, except the brown sauce and browned breadcrumbs, in a small stewpan over the fire, adding gradually sufficient brown sauce slightly to moisten the whole. Season to taste, fill the tomatoes with the preparation, sprinkle on the top of each a few browned breadcrumbs, and bake them in a moderate oven for about 15 minutes. Serve on the croûtes of fried or toasted bread, which should be round, and slightly larger than the tomatoes.

Allow 1 tomato to each person and 1 or 2 over.

TOMATOES, STUFFED, WITH MUSHROOMS.
(Tomates farcies aux champignons.)

Take 6 medium-sized tomatoes, 2 tablespoonfuls of finely-chopped mushrooms, 1 tablespoonful of breadcrumbs, ¼ of a teaspoonful of finely-chopped parsley, 1 small onion finely-chopped, 6 croûtons of fried or toasted bread, browned breadcrumbs, 1 oz. of butter, salt and pepper.

Remove the stalks of the tomatoes, and scoop out a little of the pulp. Melt the butter in a small stewpan, add to it all the ingredients except the browned breadcrumbs, and stir over the fire until thoroughly mixed. Fill the tomatoes with the preparation, sprinkle on a few browned breadcrumbs, bake in a moderate oven for 10 or 15 minutes, and serve on the croûtons.

This should be sufficient for 5 or 6 persons.

WELSH RAREBIT.

With ¼ of a lb. of Cheshire or Cheddar cheese take ½ an oz. of butter, 2 tablespoonfuls of either milk or ale, 1 teaspoonful of made mustard and some slices of hot buttered toast.

Melt the butter in a stewpan, add the cheese grated, stir until melted, then add the milk or ale gradually, mustard, and season to taste. Have ready some hot buttered toast, pour the cheese preparation on to it, and serve as hot as possible.

This should be sufficient for 3 persons.

WOODCOCK TOAST. (*See* Scotch Woodcock, p. 63.)

YORKSHIRE RABBIT OR RAREBIT.

Procure 4 oz. of Cheshire or Cheddar cheese, ½ an oz. of butter, 3 tablespoonfuls of milk or ale, some Worcester sauce or vinegar, mustard, pepper and prepare some buttered toast and 2 poached eggs.

Cut the cheese into small pieces, place them in a saucepan with the butter, milk or ale, add a little made mustard, a few drops of Worcester sauce or vinegar, pepper to taste, stir and cook gently until the mixture resembles thick cream. Meanwhile, prepare 1 slice of buttered toast, trim the edges and cut it in two, and poach the eggs in as plump a form as possible. Pour the cheese preparation over the toast, lay the eggs on the top, and serve quickly.

This should be sufficient for 2 persons.

CHAPTER III

CHEESE SAVOURIES

CAYENNE CHEESE FINGERS.

Have ready ¼ of a lb. of finely-grated cheese, ¼ of a lb. of butter, ¼ of a lb. of flour, ½ a saltspoonful of cayenne, ½ a saltspoonful of salt, and a little cold water.

Rub the butter into the flour, add the grated cheese, cayenne and salt, and mix these ingredients well together. Add sufficient cold water to mix the whole into a stiff paste, roll it out to about a ¼ of an inch in thickness, and cut the paste into fingers 3½ inches long and ¾ of an inch wide. Place them on a greased baking-sheet, and bake in a moderately cool oven until crisp and lightly browned. Serve either hot or cold.

This should be sufficient for 10 persons.

CHEESE AIGRETTES. (*See* Recipe in previous section, p. 33.)

CHEESE BALLS. (*See* Recipe, p. 34.)

CHEESE BISCUITS. (Biscuits de Fromage.)

Have ready some finely-grated cheese, puff-paste trimmings and 1 egg.

Roll the paste out thinly, sprinkle it liberally with grated cheese, and fold in three. Repeat the process twice, then cut it into rounds with a small cutter, brush them over with beaten yolk of egg, and bake in a moderately hot oven until crisp.

Allow 2 of the biscuits to each person.

CHEESE BISCUITS. (Another Method.)

Take 3 oz. of grated cheese, 2 oz. of butter, 3 oz. of flour, 1 yolk of egg, cayenne, pepper and salt.

Rub the butter into the flour, add the cheese, season to taste, and mix into a stiff dough with the yolk of egg. Roll out the dough to rather less than a $\frac{1}{4}$ of an inch in thickness, stamp it into rounds or cut it into fingers, and bake in a quick oven until crisp. The biscuits will keep for a long time in a tin, and can be heated when wanted.

Allow 2 biscuits to each person.

CHEESE BISCUITS WITH CREAM. (*See* **Recipe in Hors d'Œuvre Section, p. 12.**)

CHEESE CREAM COLD. (*See* **Recipe in Hors d'Œuvre Section, p. 12.**)

CHEESE CREAM CROÛTES. (*See* **Recipe in Hors d'Œuvre Section, p. 13.**)

CHEESE CROUSTADES. (Croustades au Fromage.)

Have ready 2 oz. of grated Cheshire or Cheddar cheese, 1 oz. of breadcrumbs, 1 tablespoonful of liquid butter, 1 tablespoonful of milk, 1 yolk of egg, a little salt, cayenne and Krona pepper, some stale bread and frying-fat.

From slices of stale bread $\frac{1}{2}$ an inch in thickness stamp out 8 or 9 croûtes $1\frac{3}{4}$ inches in diameter. Then with a smaller cutter make an inner circle, hollow the centre of each croûte to half its depth, and fry the croûtes in hot fat. Mix together in a basin the cheese, breadcrumbs, add milk, butter and egg, season well with salt and pepper, pile the preparation on the croûtes, smoothing it into a pyramidal form with a knife, brown in a quick oven, and serve as hot as possible.

This should be sufficient for 6 or 7 persons.

CHEESE D'ARTOIS. (D'Artois au Parmesan.)

Take 3 oz. of grated cheese, 1 oz. of butter, 2 yolks of eggs, 1 white of egg, salt and pepper, and about 3 or 4 oz. of puff-paste.

Beat the yolk and white of 1 egg slightly, add the cheese, butter (melted), and season rather highly with salt and pepper. Roll the paste out thinly, cut it in half, spread the preparation over one half, and cover with the other. Place it carefully on a buttered baking-tin, score it in inch-deep strips, brush over with egg, sprinkle with grated cheese, and bake for about

CHEESE SAVOURIES

10 minutes in a quick oven. When ready cut through the scores, pile on a hot dish, and serve.

This should be sufficient for 8 or 9 persons.

CHEESE FONDUE. (Fondue de Fromage.)

Procure 4 oz. of grated Gruyère or Swiss cheese, 1 oz. of butter, 1 oz. of flour, 2 yolks of eggs, $\frac{1}{4}$ of a pint of milk, a pinch of salt and a small pinch of white pepper.

Melt the butter in a stewpan, mix in the flour, add the milk, and stir and simmer gently until smooth and thick. Add the cheese, salt and pepper, and when well mixed pour the preparation on to the well-beaten yolks of eggs. Whisk and stir them lightly into the mixture. Have ready a well-buttered fondue dish or tin which the mixture should about half fill, pour it in and bake in a moderately hot oven for about 20 minutes. As the excellence of this dish depends on its lightness, it should be served the moment it is ready. Overcooking will cause it to be tough, and standing after it is cooked will make it heavy.

This should be sufficient for 6 or 7 persons.

CHEESE FRITTERS. (Beignets de Fromage.)

For the mixture take 2 tablespoonfuls of cooked macaroni, 1 tablespoonful of grated Parmesan cheese, 1 tablespoonful of thick cream or white sauce, salt and a little cayenne pepper. For the paste take some puff-paste trimmings, grated Parmesan cheese and Krona pepper. Also 1 egg, breadcrumbs or vermicelli and frying-fat.

The macaroni, after being cooked until perfectly tender, should be cut across into tiny rings, and in this condition measure 2 tablespoonfuls. Mix with it the cheese, cream or sauce, and season rather highly with salt, cayenne and pepper. Roll out the paste, sprinkle it with Parmesan cheese, add a little Krona pepper, fold it over, and roll it out again as thin as possible. Now stamp it out into rounds $1\frac{3}{4}$ inches in diameter, on half of them place a little of the mixture, and cover with the other rounds, pressing the previously wetted edges well together. Dip in egg and then in breadcrumbs or broken up vermicelli and fry in hot fat until nicely browned. Dish in a pyramidal form, sprinkle with grated cheese and Krona pepper, and serve hot.

This should be sufficient for 6 or 7 persons.

CHEESE MÉRINGUES. (Méringues au Parmesan.)

Have ready 2 whites of eggs, 2 oz. of grated Parmesan cheese, Krona pepper, cayenne, salt and frying-fat.

Whisk the whites to a very stiff froth, add a good seasoning of cayenne and a little salt to the cheese, then stir it lightly into the whisked whites. Have ready a deep pan of hot fat, drop in the preparation in small teaspoonfuls, and fry until nicely browned. Drain well, and serve sprinkled with grated Parmesan cheese and Krona pepper.

This should be sufficient for 6 or 7 persons.

CHEESE OMELET. (Omelette gratinée au Parmesan.)

Take 3 eggs, 1 tablespoonful of grated Parmesan cheese, 1 tablespoonful of cream or milk, 1 oz. of clarified butter, and a little pepper and salt.

Whisk the eggs well, then add the cheese, cream, and a little salt and pepper. Have the butter ready, heated and well skimmed, in an omelet pan, pour in the egg-mixture, and stir over the fire until the eggs begin to set. Now fold one half over the other, making it crescent-shaped, or fold the sides towards the middle in the form of a cushion. Allow the omelet to brown slightly, then turn it on to a hot dish, and serve immediately.

This should be sufficient for 2 persons.

CHEESE PATTIES. (Bouchées au Fromage.)

With 1 tablespoonful of grated Parmesan cheese take 1½ tablespoonfuls of grated Cheshire or Cheddar cheese, 1 tablespoonful of cream, 2 tablespoonfuls of thick white sauce, 1 white of egg, puff-paste, Krona pepper, cayenne and salt.

Prepare 8 patty-cases 1½ inches in diameter (*see* recipe for **Caviare Patties,** p. 33); when baked, remove and preserve the lids, scoop out the soft inside, and keep the cases hot. Stir the cream, sauce and cheese over the fire until the latter melts, then add cayenne and salt to taste, and fill the cases with the preparation. Add a little grated cheese to the stiffly-whisked white of egg, arrange it roughly in the centre of each patty, sprinkle on a little Krona pepper, and place in a moderate oven until the méringue becomes crisp and lightly browned.

This should be sufficient for 6 or 7 persons.

Note.—See also recipe for **Cheese Tartlets,** p. 77.

CHEESE SAVOURIES

CHEESE PUDDING. (Pouding au Fromage.)

To 4 oz. of grated cheese allow 1 oz. of breadcrumbs, ½ a pint of milk, 2 eggs, a little made mustard, and seasoning of salt and cayenne.

Beat the eggs slightly, and add to them the cheese, mustard, salt and pepper according to taste. Boil the milk, add it to the rest of the ingredients, pour into a buttered baking-dish in which it may be served, and bake for about 20 minutes in a brisk oven. If preferred, the mixture may be baked in small china or paper soufflé-cases, in which case only half the time should be allowed.

This should be sufficient for 5 or 6 persons.

CHEESE RAMAKINS. (Ramequins de Fromage.)

Have ready 1 oz. of Parmesan cheese, 1 oz. of Cheshire cheese, 1 oz. of butter, ½ a tablespoonful of breadcrumbs, 1 egg, milk, mace, salt and pepper to taste.

Barely cover the breadcrumbs with boiling milk, let them stand covered for 10 minutes, then pound well. Add the cheese previously grated, the butter, the yolk of the egg, season to taste, and continue the pounding until a perfectly smooth mixture is obtained. Whisk the white of egg to a stiff froth, stir it lightly into the mixture, pour it into well-buttered china or paper ramakin-cases, and bake in a quick oven until set.

This should be sufficient for 6 or 7 persons.

Note.—*See also* recipes for **Cheese Soufflé**, p. 76, and **Cheese Cream, Cold**, p. 12.

CHEESE RINGS.

Prepare some cheese paste (*see* recipe for **Cheese Straws**, p. 76).

Make the paste as directed, stamp it into rounds about 2 inches in diameter, and with a much smaller cutter remove the centre of each round. Bake them in a moderate oven, and serve hot.

This should be sufficient for 6 or 7 persons.

CHEESE SANDWICHES.

Procure some thin slices of cheese, brown bread and butter.

Cut thin slices of bread from a brown loaf at least 1 day old, and spread them liberally with butter. Cover half the prepared slices with thin slices of cheese, cover with the remaining half, and cut into squares or triangles. Place them in a moderately hot oven on a buttered baking-sheet, and when both sides of the bread are crisp and brown, arrange the sandwiches neatly on a hot dish, and serve as quickly as possible.

Allow 1 sandwich to each person and 1 or 2 over.

CHEESE SOUFFLÉ. (Soufflé au Parmesan.)

Take 3 oz. of grated Parmesan cheese, 1 oz. of butter, 1 oz. of flour, 3 whites of eggs, 2 yolks of eggs, $\frac{1}{4}$ of a pint of milk, a few grains of cayenne pepper, a little salt and some clarified butter.

Coat a soufflé-mould well with clarified butter, and tie round it a well-buttered, thickly-folded piece of paper to support the soufflé when it rises above the level of the tin. Melt the butter in a stewpan, stir in the flour, add the milk, and boil well. Now mix in, off the fire, the 2 yolks of eggs, beat well, then stir in the cheese and add seasoning to taste. Whisk the whites to a stiff froth, add them lightly to the rest of the ingredients, pour the preparation into the soufflé-tin, and bake in a hot oven from 25 to 30 minutes. Serve in the tin in which it is baked, and if not provided with an outer case, pin round it a napkin (previously warmed), and send to table quickly.

This should be sufficient for 5 or 6 persons.

CHEESE STRAWS. (Pailles au Parmesan.)

Have ready 2 oz. of butter, $2\frac{1}{2}$ oz. of flour, 2 oz. of Parmesan cheese, 1 oz. of Cheshire or Cheddar cheese, the yolk of 1 egg, a little salt, and a few grains of cayenne pepper.

Grate the cheese, mix it with the flour, rub in the butter, and season with salt and cayenne pepper. Now form into a stiff paste with the yolk of egg and cold water, adding the latter gradually until the desired consistency is obtained. Roll out thinly, cut into strips about 4 inches long and about $\frac{1}{8}$ of an inch wide, and from the trimmings stamp out some rings about $1\frac{1}{4}$ inches in diameter. Bake in a moderate oven until crisp, fill each ring with straws, and arrange them neatly on a dish, covered with a napkin or dish-paper. Serve either hot or cold.

This should be sufficient for 6 or 7 persons.

CHEESE SAVOURIES

CHEESE STRAWS. (Another Method.)

Procure 1 oz. of finely-grated cheese, 1 oz. of butter, 1 oz. of breadcrumbs, 1 oz. of flour, a good pinch of salt, a small pinch of cayenne and a little water.

Rub the butter into the flour, add the breadcrumbs, cheese, cayenne and salt, and just sufficient cold water to mix into a stiff paste. Roll the paste out to about a $\frac{1}{4}$ of an inch in thickness, cut it into strips about 3 inches long and a $\frac{1}{4}$ of an inch wide, and place the strips on a greased baking-sheet. Bake in a moderately cool oven until crisp, and serve either hot or cold.

This should be sufficient for 5 persons.

CHEESE STRAWS. (Another Method.)

With 2 oz. of grated Parmesan cheese take 4 or 5 oz. of puff-paste and a little cayenne.

Roll out the paste, using some of the cheese instead of flour for sprinkling the board, scatter cheese over the surface, fold in three and give it one turn. Repeat until the cheese is used; when rolling out for the last time sprinkle with a little cayenne pepper, and, if needed, let the paste stand for some time in a cold place after each turn. After rolling it out thinly, cut it into strips about 4 inches long and a $\frac{1}{4}$ of an inch wide, twisting each strip before placing it on a wetted baking-tin. Re-roll the trimmings, stamp out some rings $1\frac{1}{4}$ inches in diameter, and bake them with the straws until crisp and lightly browned. Arrange in bundles by means of the rings, and serve hot.

This should be sufficient for 6 or 7 persons.

CHEESE TARTLETS. (Tartelettes au Fromage.)

Take 4 oz. of grated cheese, 1 oz. of butter, 1 oz. of flour, $\frac{1}{2}$ a pint of milk, 2 or 3 eggs, salt and cayenne and puff-paste.

Melt the butter in a stewpan, stir in the flour, add the milk, and boil for 3 or 4 minutes, stirring meanwhile. Let the mixture cool slightly, stir in the yolks of eggs, cook gently for 2 or 3 minutes, but do not allow it to boil. Add the cheese, season to taste, then stir in as lightly as possible the previously stiffly-whisked whites of eggs. Have ready some patty-pans lined with thinly-rolled-out puff-paste, fill with the mixture, and bake in a quick oven.

This should be sufficient for 9 persons.

MACARONI AND CHEESE. (Macaroni au Fromage.)

With ¼ of a lb. of macaroni take 3 oz. of grated cheese, 1 oz. of butter, 2 yolks of eggs, ½ a pint of good gravy, 4 tablespoonfuls of cream, salt, cayenne and pepper.

Break the macaroni into short lengths, put them into the gravy when boiling, and simmer until tender. Strain, put the macaroni into a deep fireproof dish, and return the gravy to the stewpan. Add the well-beaten yolks of eggs, cream, salt, pepper and cayenne to taste, and stir until the mixture slightly thickens. Pour over the macaroni, sprinkle on the grated cheese, add the butter broken into small pieces, and brown with a salamander, or in a brisk oven.

This should be sufficient for 7 or 8 persons.

MACARONI CHEESE. (*See* Macaroni au Gratin, p. 49.)

TOASTED CHEESE.

Procure some cheese, butter, ale or stout, mustard and pepper, and prepare some small pieces of crisp dry toast.

To serve this dish really well either a chafing-dish or an old-fashioned cheese-toaster with an outer dish containing boiling water is needed. Cut the cheese into thin slices, place them in the cheese-toaster, spread on a little mustard, season them with pepper, and, unless the cheese is very rich, add the butter broken into small pieces. Pour over the whole 2 or 3 tablespoonfuls of ale or stout (milk may be substituted), stand the dish on a hot place or in a moderately hot oven, and cook until the cheese is melted. Serve at once in the hot-water dish, and hand crisp dry toast separately.

TOASTED CHEESE. (Another Method.)

Have ready some Cheshire or Cheddar cheese, bread, butter, mustard and pepper.

Cut the bread into slices about ½ an inch in thickness, toast them, trim off the crust, and cut each slice across into 4 squares. Cover each square with a thin slice of cheese toasted on one side, place them before a sharp fire or in a moderately hot oven, and serve as soon as sufficiently toasted.

WELSH RABBIT OR RAREBIT. (*See* Recipe in Savouries Section, p. 70.)

CHAPTER IV

EGG DISHES

ALPINE EGGS. (Œufs à la Suisse.)

With 4 eggs take 6 oz. of cheese, 2 oz. of butter, a little finely-chopped parsley, pepper and salt.

Butter a fireproof baking-dish thickly, line it with the greater part of the cheese cut in thin slices, and break the eggs over this, keeping the yolks whole. Grate the remainder of the cheese or chop it finely, and mix with it the parsley. Season the eggs liberally with salt and pepper, sprinkle over them the grated cheese, and add the remainder of the butter broken into small pieces. Bake in a quick oven for 10 minutes and serve hot.

This should be sufficient for 4 persons.

ANCHOVY EGGS. (*See* **Recipe,** p. 8.)

BAKED EGGS. (Œufs au four.)

To 6 eggs allow 2 oz. of grated cheese, 2 oz. of breadcrumbs, ½ an oz. of butter, 1 teaspoonful of chopped parsley, salt and a few grains of cayenne.

Butter 6 china or ramakin-cases, put the seasoning into them, and break an egg into each. Put an equal portion of cheese into each cup, cover with breadcrumbs, and add a small piece of butter. Bake in a moderate oven for about 5 minutes, or until set, and serve hot.

This should be sufficient for 6 persons.

BAKED EGGS À LA COQUETTE.

Procure 6 eggs, 2 oz. of finely-chopped ham or tongue, 1 oz. of butter, 6 dessertspoonfuls of cream, and seasoning of nutmeg, cayenne pepper and salt.

Liberally butter 6 ramakin-cases, divide the remainder of the butter into equal portions, and place some in each case.

To each add a dessertspoonful of cream, a pinch of nutmeg and a little salt and pepper, and place them in the oven on a baking-sheet. When the contents begin to simmer break and add the eggs carefully, place a pinch of cayenne in the centre of each yolk and replace in the oven. When sufficiently cooked sprinkle the chopped ham or tongue lightly on the white part of each egg, taking care to leave the yolk uncovered, and serve hot.

This should be sufficient for 6 persons.

BUTTERED EGGS À L'INDIENNE. (Œufs brouillés à l'Indienne.)

Have ready 3 hard-boiled eggs, 2 raw eggs, ½ an oz. of butter, curry-powder, salt and pepper, and browned bread-crumbs.

Cut the hard-boiled eggs across into rather thick slices, place them in a well-buttered gratin dish, or china baking-dish, in which they may be served, and sprinkle over them about ½ a teaspoonful of curry-powder and a few grains of cayenne. Beat the raw eggs slightly, season with salt and pepper, and pour them into the dish. Cover the surface lightly with browned breadcrumbs, put bits of butter here and there, and bake in a moderate oven for about 10 minutes.

This should be sufficient for 5 or 6 persons.

CURRIED EGGS. (Œufs au Kari.)

Take 4 hard-boiled eggs, ½ of a pint of stock or milk, 1 oz. of butter, 1 teaspoonful of curry-powder, 1 teaspoonful of flour, 1 finely-chopped small onion, lemon-juice, salt and 4 oz. of cooked rice.

Prepare the rice, shell the eggs and cut them in quarters. Fry the onion slightly in the hot butter, sprinkle in the flour and curry-powder, and cook slowly for 5 or 6 minutes. Add the stock or milk, season with salt and lemon-juice, and simmer gently for ½ an hour. Then put in the eggs, and let them remain until thoroughly heated, and serve. The rice may be arranged as a border or served separately.

This should be sufficient for 6 or 7 persons.

EGG CROQUETTES. (Croquettes aux Œufs.)

Take 4 hard-boiled eggs, 6 coarsely-chopped preserved mushrooms, 1 oz. of butter or margarine, ½ an oz. of flour, ½ a gill of milk, breadcrumbs, nutmeg, salt and pepper, frying-fat.

EGG DISHES

1. Eggs Colbert Style. 2. Eggs in Aspic. 3. Curried Eggs and Rice.

EGG DISHES

Chop the eggs finely or rub them through a wire sieve. Fry the mushrooms lightly in the hot butter, stir in the flour, add the milk, and boil well. Now put in the eggs, season to taste, add a pinch of nutmeg, mix well over the fire, then spread on a plate to cool. When ready to use shape into balls or corks, coat carefully with a batter (milk and flour mixed to the consistency of cream), cover with breadcrumbs, and fry in hot fat until golden-brown. Drain well, and serve garnished with fried parsley.

This should be sufficient for 7 or 8 persons.

EGG FRITTERS À LA MILANAISE. (Beignets d'Œufs à la Milanaise.)

With 4 hard-boiled eggs take $\frac{1}{2}$ an oz. of butter, $\frac{1}{2}$ an oz. of flour, $\frac{1}{3}$ of a pint of milk, 1 oz. of finely-chopped ham or tongue, 1 teaspoonful of finely-chopped parsley, 1 small shallot chopped and fried in butter, lemon-juice, salt, pepper, egg and breadcrumbs, frying-fat and a few sprigs of crisply-fried parsley.

Halve the eggs lengthwise, and remove the yolks, melt the butter in a stewpan, stir in the flour, add the milk, boil gently for 2 or 3 minutes. Add the chopped ham or tongue, parsley, shallot, yolks of the hard-boiled eggs, a little lemon-juice and seasoning to taste. Fill the cavities of the whites of eggs with the preparation, coat carefully with egg and breadcrumbs, and fry in hot fat until nicely browned. Drain well and serve garnished with crisply-fried parsley.

This should be sufficient for 6 or 7 persons.

EGG FRITTERS À LA ROYALE. (Beignets d'Œufs à la Royale.)

Have ready 4 eggs, 1 tablespoonful of cream, salt, pepper, frying batter (*see* **Oyster Fritters,** p. 53) and some frying-fat.

Beat the eggs, add the cream, season to taste with salt and pepper, and pour the preparation into a well-buttered plain mould. Steam gently until set, about 20 minutes, let it cool, then unmould and cut into strips about $2\frac{1}{2}$ inches long and $\frac{1}{2}$ an inch in thickness. Make the batter as directed, dip in the egg strips, and fry in hot fat until crisp and lightly browned. Drain well and serve.

This should be sufficient for 6 or 7 persons.

EGG KROMESKIS. (Cromesquis d'Œufs.)

Take 3 hard-boiled eggs, ⅛ of a pint of White sauce (p. 124), a level tablespoonful of chopped tongue or ham, ½ a teaspoonful of finely-chopped truffles, 5 thin Pancakes (*see* **Caviare Pancakes,** p. 32), salt, pepper, frying-fat.

Chop the eggs coarsely, add the sauce, tongue, truffle, seasoning to taste, and stir over the fire for a few minutes. Let the preparation cool, then divide it into pieces the size and shape of a cork, and enfold in squares of pancake. Dip separately into frying-batter, fry in hot fat until nicely browned, drain well, and serve.

This should be sufficient for 5 or 6 persons.

EGGS À LA COURTET. (Œufs à la Courtet.)

Have ready 4 tomatoes, 2 tablespoonfuls of Mayonnaise sauce (p. 122), 1 gill of aspic jelly, 2 eggs, 1½ oz. of butter, salt and pepper and some salad.

Cut the tomatoes in halves, and scoop out the centre. Have ready the eggs scrambled (as for **Scrambled Eggs,** p. 91), fill the tomatoes with the preparation, and set aside until quite cold. Coat them with cool aspic jelly, and when set, serve garnished with salad dressed with mayonnaise.

This should be sufficient for 6 or 7 persons.

EGGS À LA DIJON. (*See* Recipe, p. 16.)

EGGS À LA DREUX. (Œufs à la Dreux.)

With 4 eggs take ¼ of a lb. of lean cooked ham, ½ an oz. of butter, 1 dessertspoonful of finely-chopped parsley, 4 small rounds of buttered toast, cayenne, salt and pepper.

Chop the ham finely, and mix with it the parsley. Coat 4 deep patty-pans thickly with butter, and cover them completely with a thin layer of ham preparation. Break an egg into each pan, taking care to keep the yolk whole, sprinkle with a little cayenne pepper and salt, and add a small piece of butter. Place the patty-pans in a deep baking-tin, surround them to half their depth with boiling water, and cook them in a moderate oven until the whites are set. Have ready the rounds of toast, cut to the size of the patty-pans, dish the eggs on them, and serve.

This should be sufficient for 4 persons.

EGGS À LA MAÎTRE D'HÔTEL.

To 3 eggs allow 2 oz. of butter, 1 dessertspoonful of flour, ¼ of a pint of milk, 1 teaspoonful of chopped parsley, 1 teaspoonful of lemon-juice, and a good seasoning of salt and pepper.

Melt 1 oz. of butter in a stewpan, stir in the flour, add the milk, and boil for 2 minutes. Have ready the eggs boiled hard, remove the shells, cut each egg into 4 or 8 pieces, and arrange them neatly on a dish. Season the sauce to taste, whisk in the remainder of the butter, adding it gradually in small pieces, stir in the parsley and lemon-juice, then pour the sauce over the eggs. Send to table, and serve as quickly as possible.

This should be sufficient for 4 or 5 persons.

EGGS À LA MORNAY. (Œufs à la Mornay.)

Have ready 4 or 5 hard-boiled eggs, about 1 oz. of butter, 1½ oz. of grated cheese, ¼ of a pint of White sauce (p. 124), and a seasoning of nutmeg, salt and pepper.

Cut the eggs into thick slices, place them on a well-buttered fireproof dish, and sprinkle them lightly with nutmeg and more liberally with salt and pepper. Add 1 oz. of cheese to the sauce, pour it over the eggs. Sprinkle thickly with cheese, and add a few tiny pieces of butter. Brown the surface, about 5 minutes, in a hot oven, and serve.

This should be sufficient for 5 or 6 persons.

EGGS À LA OLIVIA. (*See* Recipe in Hors d'Œuvre Chapter, p. 16.)

EGGS À LA PIÉMONTAISE. (Œufs à la Piémontaise.)

With 6 eggs take 4 oz. of Carolina rice, 3 or 4 ripe but firm tomatoes, 2 tablespoonfuls of grated Parmesan cheese, 2 slices of bacon fried and cut into fine strips, black pepper, stock, and salt and pepper to taste.

Wash and drain the rice, cover it with stock and boil gently until soft and dry, adding more stock when necessary. Meanwhile squeeze the juice from the tomatoes and chop them finely. When the rice is ready add to it the tomatoes, bacon, cheese, and a good seasoning of salt and pepper, and press into a flat mould, which afterwards invert on to a hot dish. Fry the eggs in clarified butter or oil, trim them neatly, and arrange them in a circle round the rice shape. Place a tiny pinch of black pepper in the centre of each yolk of egg, and send to table.

This should be sufficient for 6 persons.

EGGS À LA POLONAISE. (Œufs à la Polonaise.)

To 4 or 5 eggs allow 1 tablespoonful of cream (optional), 1 teaspoonful of finely-chopped parsley, 1 teaspoonful of finely-chopped chives, 1 teacupful of small dice of bread, clarified butter, salt and pepper.

Fry the dice of bread in clarified butter and drain well. Beat the eggs, add the cream (if used), parsley, chives, fried bread and a good seasoning of salt and pepper, and pour the preparation into a stewpan containing about 2 tablespoonfuls of clarified butter. Stir over the fire until the mixture is thick enough to spread, then drop it in spoonfuls into hot clarified butter, fry, drain well, and send to table, and serve as quickly as possible.

This should be sufficient for 6 or 7 persons.

EGGS COLBERT STYLE. (Œufs à la Colbert.)

Take 4 new-laid eggs, some grated Parmesan or Gruyère cheese, salt, pepper and frying-fat or oil.

Break each egg carefully into a cup, season liberally with salt and pepper. Sprinkle over $\frac{1}{2}$ a teaspoonful of cheese, and drop carefully into hot fat or oil. Fry until they acquire a nice brown colour, 5 or 6 minutes, turning frequently with a wooden spoon meanwhile, then drain well, sprinkle liberally with cheese, and serve.

This should be sufficient for 4 persons.

EGGS IN ASPIC.

Have ready 3 hard-boiled eggs, 1 pint of aspic jelly, chervil and small cress.

Coat the bottom of six dariole-moulds with jelly, decorate them with chervil, and when set put in slices of egg and aspic jelly alternately, taking care that each layer of jelly is firmly set before adding the egg. When the whole is firmly set, unmould and decorate tastefully with chopped aspic and small cress.

This should be sufficient for 6 persons.

EGGS IN BAKED POTATOES.

With 6 eggs take 3 large potatoes, 1 oz. of grated cheese, ½ an oz. of butter, ⅓ of a pint (about) of Béchamel or White sauce (*see* **Sauces**) and breadcrumbs.

Scrub the potatoes, bake them, cut them in halves, and scoop out the greater part of the inside. Poach the eggs and trim them neatly. Put a little sauce in each halved potato, and add an egg. Mix the remainder of the sauce with half the cheese, and spread it lightly over the eggs. Sprinkle first with breadcrumbs, then with cheese, add little bits of butter, brown the surface in a hot oven, and serve.

EGGS, IN CASES. (Œufs en Caisses.)

To 6 eggs allow 1 tablespoonful of grated Parmesan cheese, 2 tablespoonfuls of breadcrumbs (about), 2 tablespoonfuls of cream (optional), 1 teaspoonful of chopped parsley, 1 finely-chopped shallot, butter, salt and pepper.

Brush the inside of 6 china or paper ramakin-cases over with clarified butter or oil, and place them on a baking-tin in the oven for a few minutes. Fry the shallot in a little butter, then drain and put it, equally divided, into the cases. To the breadcrumbs add half the cheese and parsley and a good seasoning of salt and pepper, and put an equal amount of the mixture into each case. Add a very small piece of butter, break and put in the eggs, and sprinkle with salt and pepper. Pour a little cream (if used) over each egg, add the remainder of the cheese, bake in a moderate oven until set, about 6 minutes, then sprinkle with parsley.

This should be sufficient for 6 persons.

EGGS IN GRAVY. (Œufs au Jus.)

Take 4 eggs, 2 tablespoonfuls of good gravy, walnut ketchup or some cruet sauce, browned breadcrumbs, salt and pepper.

Boil the gravy, season it with salt and pepper, add a few drops of ketchup, Worcester sauce, or whatever may be liked, and put it into 4 china soufflé-cases. Stand these in a deep baking-tin containing boiling water to half their depth, and let them remain on the stove or in the oven for 2 or 3 minutes. Now carefully break an egg into each case, add salt and pepper, sprinkle lightly with browned breadcrumbs, and cook until the eggs are set. Serve them in the cases.

This should be sufficient for 4 persons.

EGGS, STUFFED, À LA RUSSE. (*See* Recipe, p. 17.)

EGGS SUR LE PLAT.

Take 4 eggs, 1 oz. of butter and a little salt and pepper.

Spread a fireproof dish thickly with butter, break the eggs into it, taking care to keep the yolks whole, and season them lightly with salt and pepper. Put the remainder of the butter, cut into very small pieces, on the top of the eggs, and bake in a moderately hot oven until the whites become set, but not hard. Serve at once in the dish in which they were cooked.

This should be sufficient for 4 persons.

EGGS WITH BLACK BUTTER. (Œufs frits au buerre noir.)

Have ready 4 eggs, 2 oz. of butter, anchovy-paste, 1 dessertspoonful of tarragon vinegar, parsley and some well-buttered toast.

Melt the butter in a sauté-pan or frying-pan, and fry the eggs, taking care to keep the yolks whole. Have ready some well-buttered toast cut into small rounds, spread them lightly with anchovy-paste, then place the eggs on them. Re-heat the butter with the tarragon vinegar, cook it until dark brown, then pour it over the eggs and serve them garnished with fried parsley.

This should be sufficient for 4 persons.

EGGS WITH HAM. (Œufs au Jambon.)

With 6 eggs take 2 tablespoonfuls of finely-chopped cooked ham, 1 tablespoonful of browned breadcrumbs, 2 tablespoonfuls of Brown or White sauce (*see* **Sauces**), or gravy, $\frac{1}{2}$ an oz. of butter, salt, pepper and a little mushroom ketchup.

Butter 6 china soufflé-cases. Season the ham with pepper, moisten with the sauce or gravy, add a few drops of mushroom ketchup or any cruet sauce, and put the preparation into the cases. Now add the eggs, taking care to keep the yolks whole, and sprinkle on a little salt and pepper. Cover with a thin layer of breadcrumbs, place small pieces of butter on the top, bake in a moderate oven until the eggs are set, and serve them in the cases.

This should be sufficient for 6 persons.

EGG DISHES

EGGS WITH MUSHROOMS. (Œufs aux Champignons.)

Procure 6 eggs, 12 small mushrooms, 1 oz. of butter, 2 small onions, ½ a pint of good gravy, pepper and salt.

Boil the eggs hard, and when cold cut them into rather thin slices. Slice, and fry the mushrooms and onions in the butter, add the gravy, bring to the boil, and season to taste. Put in the sliced eggs, let them become thoroughly hot, then dish carefully, and serve.

This should be sufficient for 7 or 8 persons.

EGGS WITH PARMESAN. (Œufs au Parmesan.) (*See* Alpine Eggs, p. 79.)

EGGS WITH TONGUE. (Langue de Bœuf aux Œufs.)

Take 4 eggs, 4 slices of cooked tongue, 2 or 3 tablespoonfuls of good gravy, a piece of meat glaze the size of a small walnut, lemon-juice, salt and pepper.

Put the slices of tongue into a sauté-pan or stewpan, with the gravy and glaze, make thoroughly hot, and season to taste. Poach the eggs in boiling water, slightly salted and flavoured with lemon-juice and trim them to a round shape. Place the eggs on the slices of tongue, and trim the edges if necessary, arrange on a hot dish, strain the gravy over, and serve.

This should be sufficient for 4 persons.

EGGS WITH WHITE SAUCE. (Œufs à la Tripe.)

With 6 eggs take ½ a pint of good White sauce (p. 124), a little finely-chopped parsley and 2 tablespoonfuls of cream.

Boil the eggs hard, let them remain in water until quite cold, then divide each one into slices or small sections. Make the sauce as directed, season it with salt and pepper, and add the cream. Arrange the prepared eggs in 6 china coquille-cases, or in 1 dish, cover them with sauce, sprinkle lightly with parsley, then serve.

This should be sufficient for 6 persons.

FRICASSÉE OF EGGS. (Fricassée d'Œufs.)

Have ready 4 hard-boiled eggs, ½ a pint of White sauce (p. 124), 7 or 8 fried or toasted croûtons of bread, chopped parsley, salt and pepper.

Boil the eggs hard, cut them into rather thick slices, and

reserve the yolk of 1 for garnishing. Prepare the sauce as directed, season to taste, put in the sliced eggs, and let them become thoroughly hot. Arrange neatly on a hot dish, sprinkle with parsley, and yolk of egg previously passed through a fine sieve, garnish with the croûtons of fried or toasted bread, then serve.

This should be sufficient for 4 or 5 persons.

OVERTURNED EGGS.

Procure 6 eggs and have ready some breadcrumbs, butter, salt and pepper.

Thoroughly butter some china ramakin-cases or very small patty-pans. Coat them rather thickly with breadcrumbs, into each one break an egg, and sprinkle lightly with salt and pepper. Bake gently until set, then invert them carefully on to a hot dish, and serve.

This should be sufficient for 6 persons.

OX EYES.

Have ready 6 eggs, some stale bread, sour cream, milk and butter.

Cut some slices of stale bread $\frac{3}{4}$ of an inch in thickness. Toast and stamp them into rounds 3 inches in diameter, then take out the middle of each round with a $1\frac{1}{2}$-inch diameter cutter. Place the rings in a well-buttered fireproof dish, pour over them gradually as much sour cream as they will absorb without becoming sodden, then break 1 egg carefully into each ring. Sprinkle lightly with salt and pepper, cover each egg with 1 teaspoonful of new milk, and bake gently until the whites are set, but not hard.

This should be sufficient for 6 persons.

PARMENTIER EGGS. (Œufs à la Parmentier.) (*See* Eggs in Baked Potatoes, p. 85.)

PLOVERS' EGGS. (Œufs de Pluviers.)

Plovers' eggs are served boiled hard. They are often used to garnish salads. The eggs are usually boiled from 15 to 20 minutes; and the albumen after boiling obtains a beautiful translucent bluish colour.

Allow 1 egg for each person.

PLOVERS' EGGS IN ASPIC. (Œufs de Pluviers en Aspic.)

Take 6 hard-boiled plovers' eggs, aspic jelly, salad, chilli and truffle for decoration.

Set a little aspic jelly in the bottom of the darioles chosen, and decorate them tastefully with chilli and fancifully-cut truffle. Place 1 egg in each mould, fill up with aspic jelly, and put on ice or in a cold place until set. Unmould and serve tastefully garnished with salad.

Allow 1 egg for each person.

PLOVERS' EGGS ON CROÛTES. (Œufs de Pluviers sur Croûtes.)

Procure 6 plovers' eggs and have ready some brown bread, butter, salad and aspic jelly.

Cut some moderately-thin slices of bread and butter, and stamp out some small rounds. Work about 2 oz. of butter until creamy, and put it into a paper cone. Boil the plovers' eggs hard and let them get cold, place 1 egg on each round of bread and butter, and keep it in place by forcing some of the butter round the egg. Garnish with chopped aspic and salad. Variety may be introduced by using Anchovy or Montpelier butter (pp. 102 and 104).

Allow 1 egg for each person.

POACHED EGGS. (Œufs pochés.)

Have ready some eggs, buttered toast, salt and vinegar, or lemon-juice.

Eggs for poaching should be fresh, but not new-laid; for if poached before they have been laid 36 hours, the white is so milky that it is almost impossible to coagulate it. To prepare, boil some water in a shallow stewpan or deep frying-pan, add salt to taste, and allow to each pint of water 1 tablespoonful of vinegar, or 1 teaspoonful of lemon-juice. Break the egg into a cup, taking care to keep the yolk whole, and when the water boils, remove the pan to the side of the fire, and gently slip the egg into it. Tilt the pan, with a tablespoon gently fold the white of the egg over the yolk, so as to produce a plump appearance, and simmer gently until the white is set. Take it up carefully with a slice, trim the edges, and serve either on buttered toast, slices of ham or bacon, or spinach.

POACHED EGGS WITH HAM. (Œufs à la Dreux.)

With 4 eggs take 3 oz. of finely-chopped cooked ham, 4 rounds of buttered toast the size of the eggs when cooked, 4 small teaspoonfuls of cream or milk, butter, 1 teaspoonful of finely-chopped parsley, cayenne, salt and pepper.

Add the parsley and a little pepper to the ham. Coat 4 small deep patty-pans thickly with butter, over which sprinkle the ham preparation, then to each patty-pan add an egg, breaking them carefully so as to keep the yolks whole. Season with salt, pepper and cayenne, add a teaspoonful of cream to each tin, and place on the top a morsel of butter. Put the tins in the oven, in a sauté-pan, surround them to half their depth with boiling water, and poach until the white is firm. When ready, turn the eggs carefully out of the tins on to the toast, and serve.

This should be sufficient for 4 persons.

POACHED EGGS WITH SPINACH. (Œufs pochés aux Epinards.)

Have ready 6 eggs, 1 pint of spinach purée either fresh or tinned, 1 oz. of butter, 1 tablespoonful of Brown sauce (p. 121), 1 teaspoonful of lemon-juice or vinegar, nutmeg, salt, pepper, and a few sippets of toasted bread.

Prepare the Spinach purée, place it in a saucepan, add the butter, a good pinch of nutmeg, salt, pepper and the brown sauce, and make thoroughly hot. Meanwhile poach the eggs and trim them neatly. Turn the spinach on to a hot dish, flatten the surface lightly; upon it place the eggs and garnish with the sippets. Serve brown sauce separately.

This should be sufficient for 6 persons.

POACHED EGGS WITH TOMATO SAUCE. (Œufs pochés à la Tomate.)

Procure 6 eggs, 4 oz. of rice, 1 oz. of butter, $\frac{1}{4}$ of a pint of Tomato sauce (p. 124), $\frac{1}{2}$ a pint of stock, salt and pepper.

Wash and drain the rice, add it to the boiling stock, cook gently until all the stock has become absorbed, leaving the rice soft and dry, then stir in the butter and season to taste. Poach the eggs until firm and trim them neatly. Arrange the rice lightly on a hot dish, place the eggs upon it, and pour the hot sauce round and serve.

This should be sufficient for 6 persons.

EGG DISHES

SAVOURY EGGS.

Take 4 eggs, 4 small rounds of buttered toast, 2 oz. of chopped cooked ham, 1 teaspoonful of finely-chopped parsley, and a little salt and pepper.

Butter 4 small china ramakin-cases or dariole-moulds, and coat them thickly with ham and parsley previously mixed together. Break an egg carefully into each case, and sprinkle them with salt and pepper. Bake or steam until firm, then turn them on to the prepared toast, and serve.

This should be sufficient for 4 persons.

SCOTCH EGGS. (Œufs Écossaise.)

Prepare 3 hard-boiled eggs and take ½ lb. sausage meat, 1 egg, breadcrumbs, frying-fat and 6 croûtes of fried bread.

Let the eggs become quite cold, remove the shells, and cover each one completely with sausage-meat. Coat them carefully with beaten egg and breadcrumbs, and fry in hot fat until nicely browned. Cut each egg in half, dish them cut side upwards on the croûtes of fried bread besprinkled with chopped parsley, and serve either hot or cold.

This should be sufficient for 6 persons.

SCRAMBLED EGGS. (Œufs brouillés.)

Have ready 4 eggs, 3 slices of buttered toast, 1 oz. of butter, 2 tablespoonfuls of cream or milk, salt and pepper, and a little finely-chopped parsley.

If liked, round, oval, or triangular croûtes of toasted bread may be used, but for ordinary purposes each slice of toast may be trimmed and cut into quarters. Beat the eggs slightly, season them with salt and pepper, add the cream or milk, and pour the mixture into a stewpan, in which the butter should have been previously melted. Stir over the fire until the eggs begin to set, then pile on the toast, sprinkle with parsley and serve.

This should be sufficient for 5 or 6 persons.

SCRAMBLED EGGS AND HAM. (Œufs brouillés au Jambon.)

Take 2 tablespoonfuls of finely-chopped ham, 2 eggs, 1 oz. of butter, 1 tablespoonful of milk, salt and pepper and 2 rounds of buttered toast.

Melt the butter in a stewpan, put in the ham and let it heat gradually in the butter. Beat the eggs, add the milk, season to taste, pour it into the stewpan, and stir until the eggs begin to set. Have the hot toast ready and cut into quarters, pile the preparation lightly upon it, and serve at once. Tongue or other kinds of meat may be substituted for ham.

This should be sufficient for 3 or 4 persons.

SCRAMBLED EGGS WITH ANCHOVIES. (*See* Recipe, p. 38.)

SCRAMBLED EGGS WITH GREEN PEA PURÉE. (Œufs à la St. Germaine.)

With 6 eggs take ⅓ of a pint of green pea purée, 1½ oz. of butter, 1 tablespoonful of either Brown or White sauce (*see* Sauces), 2 tablespoonfuls of milk, salt, pepper and chopped parsley.

Obtain the purée by passing cooked green peas through a fine sieve, place it in a stewpan, add ½ an oz. of butter, the sauce and seasoning to taste, and make thoroughly hot. Melt the remainder of the butter in another stewpan, add the eggs, previously beaten, seasoned to taste, and mixed with the milk, and stir over the fire until the mixture is sufficiently cooked. Place the green pea purée in 8 or 9 small well-buttered ramakin cases, fill them with the egg mixture, sprinkle with parsley, and serve.

This should be sufficient for 8 or 9 persons.

SCRAMBLED EGGS WITH MUSHROOMS. (Œufs brouillés aux Champignons.)

Have ready 4 eggs, 6 button mushrooms (preferably fresh ones), 1 oz. of butter, 2 tablespoonfuls of cream or milk, 2 slices of buttered toast, salt and pepper.

Prepare the mushrooms, cut them into small dice, and fry lightly in the butter. Meanwhile trim the toast and divide each slice into 4 squares. Beat the eggs slightly, season them with salt and pepper, add the cream, and pour the mixture into the stewpan. Stir over the fire until the eggs begin to set, then pile the preparation on the toast, and serve as hot as possible.

This should be sufficient for 6 persons.

CHAPTER V

SANDWICHES

The term Sandwich was originally applied to slices of meat placed between bread and butter, but it has now a much wider meaning, for it is used to describe an endless number of pounded and shredded preparations, the varieties being multiplied by the addition of savoury butter, sauces, and condiments unknown in the eighteenth century when sandwiches were first introduced. The old comparatively substantial form still accompanies the sportsman and traveller, but those intended for " afternoon tea " are dainty trifles, pleasing the eye and palate, but too flimsy to allay hunger where it exists.

To have sandwiches in perfection the bread should not be more than one day old, and sandwich loaves should be provided when a large number have to be prepared, or large French rolls, when rolled sandwiches are preferred. Creamed butter (p. 102) is more easily spread than ordinary butter, but when the latter is used it should first be beaten to a cream. Savoury anchovy, lobster, prawn, and shrimp butters (*see* recipes, pp. 102-104) may be usefully employed to give piquancy and variety to other substances ; they are also used alone in the preparation of rolled sandwiches, which consist of single slices of bread and butter, spread with some prepared substance, and then lightly rolled.

Sandwiches for any occasion where they will come in contact with gloved fingers should be left perfectly plain on the outside, but when they may be eaten with a fork some pretty effects may be produced by decorating them with variously-coloured chaud-froid sauces. Or, if preferred, they may be decorated with cold aspic jelly, and garnished with lobster coral, Krona pepper, tiny sprigs of parsley or watercress, small salad, hard-boiled yolk or white of egg, etc.

The shape of sandwiches matters little; they may be cut into square, oblong, round, or crescent shapes. They should be dished up on lace paper, or on a folded napkin, and arranged in a row or circle, so that each piece of sandwich overlaps the other.

Where a variety of sandwiches is served, it is advisable to place a neatly-written label, indicating the name of the sandwich, on each dish.

The best way to keep sandwiches fresh and moist is to place a damp napkin over them until they are required for table.

SANDWICHES

ADELAIDE SANDWICHES.

Have ready some cooked chicken and ham, thin slices of white bread and Curry-butter (p. 103).

Cut the chicken and ham into very thin slices, and remove all skin, gristle, and the greater part of the fat. Prepare some thin slices of bread, spread with curry-butter, add next a slice of ham, then a layer of chicken, sprinkle lightly with salt, and cover with bread and butter. Press well to make the parts adhere firmly together, trim away the crusts, and cut into 4 triangles. Dish neatly on a folded napkin, and garnish with watercress or parsley.

ALEXANDRA SANDWICHES.

Take $\frac{1}{2}$ a lb. of finely-chopped chicken or game, $\frac{1}{4}$ of a lb. of finely-chopped ham, 1 tablespoonful of mushrooms cut into dice, 1 tablespoonful of truffles cut into dice, $\frac{1}{2}$ an oz. of meat glaze, 1 or 2 sheets or equivalent amount of packet gelatine, about $\frac{1}{4}$ pint of Brown sauce (p. 121), a good seasoning of salt and pepper, a loaf of bread and some creamed or watercress butter.

Put 3 or 4 tablespoonfuls of brown sauce, the glaze and gelatine into a stewpan, and when the whole is reduced to a liquid state add the chicken or game, ham, mushroom, and truffles. Season to taste, stir over the fire until thoroughly hot, then turn into a square mould. When cold cut into thin slices, place them between slices of bread and butter, trim the edges neatly, and cut into 4 triangles or squares.

SANDWICHES

ANCHOVY AND EGG SANDWICHES.

With 10 anchovies take 3 hard-boiled yolks of eggs, 2 tablespoonfuls of grated Parmesan cheese, butter, a few grains of cayenne, white or brown bread and some Curry-butter (p. 103).

Wash and bone the anchovies, pound them in a mortar with the yolks of eggs, cheese, as much butter as is needed to moisten the whole, and a little cayenne. Prepare some thin slices of bread and curry-butter, spread half of them with the preparation, cover with the remainder, and press these well together. Next trim the edges neatly, and cut them into triangles or any shape preferred. Dish neatly on a folded napkin or lace paper, and serve garnished with watercress or parsley.

BEEF SANDWICHES.

Have ready some cold roast beef, tomato, cucumber or cress, mustard or Curry-butter (p. 103), white bread and salt.

Spread thin slices of bread with mustard or curry-butter, cover half of them with thinly-sliced beef, add slices of tomato, cucumber, or watercress leaves, seasoned with salt, pepper and vinegar. Cover with buttered bread, press well together, trim and cut into squares or triangles. Variety may be obtained by spreading the bread with creamed butter, and adding a thin layer of Horseradish sauce to the beef instead of tomato or cucumber.

BLOATER SANDWICHES.

Procure 2 or 3 bloaters and take some butter, pepper and salt, white or brown bread and watercress-butter.

Grill or fry the bloaters, remove all the skin and bone, and chop them finely. If available, pound them in a mortar until smooth: otherwise beat well, and add butter until a soft smooth paste is formed. Pass through a wire sieve, season to taste with pepper and salt, spread on thin slices of bread, and cover with bread coated thickly with Watercress-butter (p. 104). Trim away the crusts, and cut into circles, squares or triangles.

BUTTER. (Savoury butter for Sandwiches.) (*See* Recipes, p. 102.)

CAVIARE SANDWICHES.

Take some Russian caviare, creamed butter, lemon-juice, cayenne pepper and thin slices of bread.

Prepare the slices of bread, spread them lightly with caviare, sprinkle with lemon-juice and a little cayenne. Have ready an equal number of slices of bread and Creamed butter (p. 102), cover, press lightly together, trim, and cut into square, triangular, or finger-shaped pieces. These sandwiches may be varied by using lobster, prawn, or shrimp-butter, any of which flavours combine agreeably with that of caviare.

CHEESE SANDWICHES.

Have ready some Cheshire or Cheddar cheese, butter, anchovy-essence or paste, white or brown bread, salt and pepper, cayenne.

Grate the cheese finely, then either pound or work it until smooth with a little seasoning, anchovy-essence or paste, and as much butter as is needed to form the whole into a soft paste. Have ready some thin slices of bread and butter, spread the cheese preparation on half of them, cover with the remainder, press well, trim and shape.

CHICKEN MAYONNAISE SANDWICHES.

With some cold cooked chicken or ham have ready some Mayonnaise sauce (p. 122), watercress, or mustard and cress and very small rolls.

Wash and dry the cress thoroughly, and remove the stalks. Shred the chicken and ham finely, season with pepper, and moisten with mayonnaise sauce. Scoop the crumb from the rolls, put in a little of the chicken mixture, add a layer of cress, then a little more chicken mixture, and replace the lid. Nearly all the mixtures for spreading on bread may be used as a filling for rolls.

CHICKEN (OR CHICKEN AND HAM) SANDWICHES.

Have ready some cooked chicken, cooked ham or tongue, creamed or watercress butter and 1 large French roll or white bread.

Select a roll 1 day old, rasp the crust, but do not remove it, slice thinly, and spread with butter. Shred the chicken and ham or tongue finely, place a layer between 2 slices of

SANDWICHES

1. Chicken and Ham Sandwiches. 2. Cheese Sandwiches.
3. Cucumber Sandwiches.

bread and butter, and press well together. Arrange overlapping each other in a circle on a folded napkin, and serve garnished with small salad or watercress.

COD'S ROE SANDWICHES.

Procure some cod's roe and liver, and have ready some brown bread, butter, essence of anchovy, 1 finely-chopped small onion, 1 teaspoonful of finely-chopped parsley, lemon-juice or vinegar, salt and pepper.

Fry the onion in $\frac{1}{2}$ an oz. of butter until lightly browned, add the roe and liver, cut up small, the parsley and seasoning to taste. Stir over the fire for a few minutes, then pound, sieve, and spread it when cold on brown bread and butter. Press well, trim, and cut into circles, squares or triangles. Dish tastefully, and serve garnished with watercress or parsley.

CUCUMBER SANDWICHES.

With 1 large cucumber take some creamed butter, white or brown bread, salad-oil, lemon-juice or vinegar, salt and pepper.

Peel the cucumber, slice it thinly, season liberally with salt, drain on a hair sieve for 1 hour, and dry thoroughly. Now put it into a basin and sprinkle with pepper, salad-oil, lemon-juice, or vinegar, liberally or otherwise according to taste. Have ready some thin slices of bread and butter, stamp out some rounds of suitable size, place slices of cucumber between 2 rounds of bread, and press the parts well together. Dish slightly overlapping each other in a circle on a folded napkin, and serve garnished with parsley.

EGG AND GHERKIN SANDWICHES.

Take 3 eggs, 1 or 2 pickled gherkins, butter, white or brown bread, creamed butter, salt and pepper.

Boil the eggs for 15 minutes, let them remain in water until quite cold, then remove the shells, and chop the whites finely. If available, pound the yolks of the eggs in a mortar with sufficient butter to form a moist paste. Or, work together in a basin until smooth and moist, then season to taste with salt and pepper. Spread some thin slices of bread and butter with the yolk of egg preparation, sprinkle lightly with chopped white of egg, and add a few very thin strips of gherkin. Cover with more bread and butter, press well together, trim off the crusts, and cut into circles, squares, or triangles. Dish neatly on a folded napkin, or lace paper, and serve garnished with parsley.

EGG SANDWICHES.

Procure some fresh eggs, watercress, or mustard and cress, white or brown bread, butter, oil, vinegar, salt and pepper.

Boil the eggs for 15 minutes, then crack the shells, and leave the eggs in water until quite cold. When ready, shell, slice them thinly, season with salt and pepper, and sprinkle lightly with oil and vinegar mixed in equal proportions. Let them remain for 15 minutes, then turn them carefully and season and sprinkle as before. Meanwhile wash and dry the cress thoroughly, and season it with oil, vinegar, salt and pepper. Cut some thin slices of bread and butter, spread half of them with the prepared eggs and the rest with cress, press them firmly together, trim away the crust, and cut into shape. Dish them neatly on a folded napkin, garnished with small salad or watercress.

FOIE-GRAS SANDWICHES.

With 1 tin or terrine of foie-gras take some bread and butter.

Prepare some thin slices of bread and butter, on half of them spread slices of foie-gras, and cover with the remainder. Press the parts firmly together, trim the edges neatly, and cut them into square, triangular, or finger-shaped pieces. Arrange them neatly on a daintily-covered dish, and garnish with watercress or parsley.

FOIE-GRAS SANDWICHES, IMITATION.

Have ready $\frac{1}{2}$ a lb. of calf's liver, $\frac{1}{4}$ of a lb. of bacon, 1 small carrot, 1 small onion, a bouquet-garni (parsley, thyme, bay-leaf), salt and pepper, nutmeg, bread and butter.

Cut the bacon and liver into small pieces, and slice the carrot and onion thinly. Fry the bacon for 2 or 3 minutes, then put in the liver, carrot, onion, herbs, and a good pinch of nutmeg. Season to taste with salt and pepper, cook gently for about 10 minutes, then pound in a mortar until smooth, and rub through a wire sieve. Now add the butter or cream gradually until a soft paste is obtained, spread it rather thickly between slices of bread and butter, press well together, trim, and cut into round, triangular, or finger-shaped pieces. Dish neatly on a napkin garnished with small salad, watercress, or parsley.

OLIVE SANDWICHES. (*See* **Recipe in Hors d'Œuvres Section,** p. 21.)

OYSTER SANDWICHES.

With 12 oysters finely chopped take $\frac{1}{2}$ an oz. of butter, 1 teaspoonful of very fine breadcrumbs, 2 tablespoonfuls of cream, $\frac{1}{2}$ a well-beaten egg, salt and pepper to taste.

Stir the ingredients over the fire for a few minutes, then turn the preparation into a small mould, and, when cold, slice thinly, and serve between very thin well-buttered brown bread.

PRINCESS SANDWICHES.

To 6 oz. of cooked chicken allow 3 oz. of cooked ham or tongue, 1 tablespoonful of grated cheese, 2 hard-boiled yolks of eggs, oil, vinegar, mustard, salt and pepper, and some white bread and butter.

Chop the chicken and ham finely, pound them in a mortar with the cheese and yolks of eggs, adding vinegar, mustard, salt and pepper to taste, and as much oil as is needed to moisten the whole. Place the preparation between thin slices of bread and butter, press well, trim neatly, and cut into circles, squares, triangles, or fingers, as may be preferred.

ROLLED SANDWICHES.

Have ready 6 oz. of finely-chopped cooked chicken, 2 oz. of finely-chopped ham or tongue, 2 tablespoonfuls of Mayonnaise sauce (p. 122), and some brown bread.

Pound the chicken and ham or tongue in a mortar until smooth, adding a little liquid butter to facilitate the process. Season to taste, and rub through a fine sieve, then stir in the mayonnaise sauce. Cut some thin slices of bread and butter, trim off the crusts, spread them with this preparation, roll up firmly, wrap them lightly in a clean cloth, and let them remain in a cool place for 1 hour. Dish them daintily on a folded napkin or lace paper, and serve garnished with small cress.

SALAD SANDWICHES.

Procure some lettuce, watercress, mustard and cress, and have ready some Mayonnaise sauce (p. 122), white or brown bread, butter, and salt.

Wash and dry the lettuce and cress thoroughly, then shred the lettuce finely, remove the stalks from the cress, season with salt, and mix with the mayonnaise sauce. Place a layer of this preparation between thin slices of bread and butter, press them well together, trim away the crusts, and cut into desired shapes.

SALMON SANDWICHES.

Take some cold boiled salmon, prepared cucumber (*see* **Cucumber Sandwiches**), mayonnaise or tartare sauce, and bread and butter.

Cover thin slices of bread and butter with salmon separated into very small flakes, add a thin layer of mayonnaise or tartare sauce, and on the top place slices of cucumber. Cover with more bread and butter, press well together, trim, and cut into shape. Other kinds of fish may be used in this manner, or they may be pounded and passed through a sieve. Tomato, lettuce, or cress may replace the cucumber, and any suitable thick sauce may be substituted for the mayonnaise or tartare sauce.

SARDINE AND TOMATO SANDWICHES.

To 1 tin of sardines allow 2 hard-boiled yolks of eggs, 2 or 3 firm tomatoes, lemon-juice or vinegar, salt and pepper, and some white or brown bread and butter.

Skin and bone the sardines, and split them in halves. Pass the tomatoes and yolks of eggs through a fine sieve, mix with them a little butter, add the lemon-juice or vinegar, and salt and pepper to taste. Prepare some fingers of bread, spread them with the tomato preparation; on the top place $\frac{1}{2}$ a sardine, and cover with fingers of bread and butter. Press well together, and dish tastefully on a folded napkin garnished with parsley.

SARDINE BUTTER SANDWICHES.

With 1 tin of sardines take 1 or 2 French rolls, butter, lemon-juice, Krona pepper, and white pepper.

Skin and bone the sardines, rub them through a fine sieve, add lemon-juice, Krona pepper, and white pepper to taste, and work them to a soft paste with a little butter. Rasp the rolls well, but do not remove the crusts; cut them into thin slices, spread them with the fish preparation, and roll up lightly. If convenient, wrap them compactly in a clean cloth, and let them remain in a cold place for 1 hour before serving.

SPORTSMAN'S SANDWICHES.

Take some cold game, chicken or meat, white bread, plain or creamed butter, Tartare sauce (p. 124), and French mustard.

Toast some ¼-inch slices of bread lightly, split them, and butter the plain sides. On half of them place thin slices of game, chicken, or meat, spread on a little tartare sauce seasoned with French mustard, and cover with more bread and butter. Press well, trim neatly, and cut into squares. If to be packed, wrap them in lettuce leaves, and finally in greaseproof paper.

ST. JAMES'S SANDWICHES.

Prepare some puff-paste, finely-chopped cooked game or chicken, finely-chopped ham or tongue, and take some cream, butter, lemon-juice, 1 egg, salt and pepper.

Roll the paste out to about ¾ of an inch in thickness, and cut it into oblong shapes 2½ inches long and 1¼ inches wide. Brush them over with yolk of egg, and bake in a hot oven. While they are cooking moisten the game or chicken, etc., with a little butter and cream, add a few drops of lemon-juice, and season to taste with salt and pepper. When the paste is ready remove the tops with a sharp knife, scoop out the soft inside, and fill with the preparation. Brush the edges over with white of egg, replace the tops, and return to the oven for a few minutes to set the filling and seal the edges. Serve either hot or cold.

SWEDISH SANDWICHES.

Have ready some cream cheese, ½ a gill of Mayonnaise sauce (p. 122), 1 gherkin, 6 olives, 1 teaspoonful of capers, bread and butter.

Chop the gherkin, olives, and capers finely, and mix with them the mayonnaise sauce. Cut some thin slices of bread and butter, spread half of them with the preparation, and the remainder with cream cheese. Press one of each kind well together, arrange them tastefully on a folded napkin or dish-paper, and serve garnished with small salad.

TOMATO SANDWICHES.

Procure some ripe firm tomatoes, creamed butter, white or brown bread, lemon-juice or vinegar, salt and pepper.

Pour boiling water over the tomatoes, let them remain immersed for 2 minutes, then drain and cover with cold water. Allow them to become quite cold, dry well, remove the skins and slice thinly. Season with salt and pepper, and sprinkle with lemon-juice or vinegar, sparingly or otherwise, according to taste. Have ready some thin slices of bread and butter, stamp out some rounds of suitable size, place slices of tomato between 2 rounds of bread, and press well to make the parts adhere firmly together. Serve garnished with small salad.

SAVOURY BUTTER FOR SANDWICHES

ANCHOVY BUTTER. (Beurre d'Anchois.)

With $\frac{1}{4}$ of a lb. of butter take 3 anchovies or 1 teaspoonful of essence and a few grains of cayenne.

Wash and bone the anchovies, pound them well in a mortar, and rub them through a fine hair sieve. Mix the paste thus obtained smoothly with the butter, add cayenne to taste, and use as required. When anchovy-essence is used, it is mixed smoothly with the butter.

CREAMED BUTTER.

To $\frac{1}{2}$ a lb. of fresh butter allow 1 gill of cream, mustard, salt and pepper, and a few grains of cayenne.

Beat the butter to a cream, whip the cream stiffly, then add it lightly to the butter, and season to taste with mustard, salt, pepper, or cayenne.

CURLED BUTTER.

Tie a strong cloth by two of the corners to an iron hook in the wall. Tie the other end of the cloth into a knot, but so loosely that the index finger may be easily passed through it. Place the butter in the cloth, twist it lightly, thus forcing

SANDWICHES

the butter through the knot in fine short rolls or curls. The butter may then be garnished with parsley and served. Butter for garnishing hams, etc., should be worked until sufficiently soft, and then used by means of a piece of stiff paper folded in the form of a cornet. The butter is squeezed in fine strings through the hole at the bottom of the cornet.

CURRY BUTTER.

Take 4 oz. of fresh butter, 1 heaped teaspoonful of curry-powder, ½ a teaspoonful of lemon-juice, and salt to taste.

Beat the butter to a cream, then stir in the curry-powder and lemon-juice, and add salt to taste.

FAIRY OR FEATHERY BUTTER.

Work the butter until it is sufficiently soft, then place it in a piece of coarse butter muslin or some loosely woven fabric through which it can be forced in fine particles, and which must be previously wetted with cold water. Draw the edges of the muslin together and press the butter gently through, letting it fall lightly into the dish in which it will be served, or round any dish it is intended to garnish.

GREEN BUTTER.

With 4 oz. of fresh butter take 1½ tablespoonfuls of finely-chopped washed parsley, 1 tablespoonful of lemon-juice, anchovy-essence or paste, salt and pepper.

Beat the butter to a cream, add the parsley, lemon-juice, and anchovy-essence or paste to taste, season with salt and pepper, and when thoroughly mixed, use as required.

HAM BUTTER.

To 4 oz. of finely-chopped lean cooked ham allow 2 oz. of butter, 1 tablespoonful of thick cream, pepper and cayenne.

Pound the ham in a mortar until smooth, adding gradually a little butter. Pass through a fine sieve, work in the cream and the rest of the butter, season to taste, and use as required.

LOBSTER BUTTER. (Beurre de Homard.)

Have ready some lobster coral, butter, cayenne and salt.

Dry the coral thoroughly, then pound it until smooth, adding cayenne and salt to taste, and a little butter gradually until the desired consistency is attained.

MAÎTRE D'HÔTEL BUTTER.

Take 1 oz. butter, 1 teaspoonful of finely-chopped parsley, and 1 teaspoonful of lemon-juice, and salt and pepper to taste.

Mix the ingredients well together and spread on a plate. When firm and cold use as required.

MONTPELIER BUTTER. (Beurre Montpelier.)

Procure some watercress, fresh butter, pepper and salt.

Choose fresh young watercress, strip the leaves from the stalks, wash and dry them thoroughly, and chop them finely. Enclose the chopped cress in the corner of a clean cloth, dip it 2 or 3 times into cold water, then squeeze as dry as possible. Knead it into the butter, adding it by degrees until the butter is sufficiently green, then add salt and pepper to taste, and use as required.

MOULDED BUTTER.

Butter may be shaped without the aid of moulds, but round butter-moulds or wooden stamps are much used and are made in a variety of patterns. They should be kept scrupulously clean, and before the butter is pressed in, the moulds should be scalded, and afterwards well soaked in cold water. The butter at once takes the impress of the mould, and may therefore be turned out immediately into the butter-dish. In hot weather a little ice should be placed either round or beneath the butter-dish. Dishes with a double bottom are constructed for this purpose.

MUSTARD BUTTER.

Take 4 oz. of fresh butter, 1 teaspoonful of made mustard, and a little salt.

Beat the butter to a cream, then mix in the mustard, and add salt to taste.

WATERCRESS BUTTER. (*See* Recipe above for Montpelier Butter.)

CHAPTER VI

SALADS

Salads.—Although lettuce frequently forms the foundation of salads composed of raw materials, there are few vegetables and edible plants that may not be used for the purpose. The long list of those generally regarded as most appropriate includes artichokes, asparagus, beetroot, carrots, cauliflower, cresses, cucumbers, endive, French beans, lentils, lettuce, onions, potatoes, radishes, salsify, spinach, tomatoes, walnuts, and many other products. On the Continent, numerous tempting salads are prepared from cold cooked vegetables, which in England are rarely utilized in this manner; but a typical French salad is composed entirely of one vegetable, for the cooks of that nation will on no account mix any two vegetables or salad plants. By these means, the characteristic delicate flavour of choice vegetables is preserved; hence the superiority of salads prepared by them. As compounding salads is regarded as an art that only a few specially gifted excel in, ordinary cooks cannot be expected to attain perfection in this respect, but careful attention to a few simple details should enable them to prepare at least a palatable dish. To ensure success, it is absolutely necessary that the plants and vegetables employed should be young, freshly gathered, and crisp. If stale and limp, they may be freshened by immersion in cold water for a time, otherwise it is better simply to wash them thoroughly. Probably the point upon which perfection largely depends is the more or less complete removal of moisture after washing. When a salad basket is not available, the materials should be well drained and shaken in a colander, and afterwards in a clean dry cloth held by the corners, and shaken lightly until the salad is dry. Lettuce should always be torn into shreds, not cut with a knife; and it is a good plan to pour the salad dressing into the bottom of the bowl, lay the vegetables upon it, and mix vigorously at the moment of serving. Salads afford considerable scope for the exercise of individual taste and inventive faculty, and whatever their composition, they should always look cool, inviting, and dainty.

SALADS

ANCHOVY SALAD. (Salade d'Anchois.) (*See* **Spanish Sardine Salad, p. 117.**)

Substitute anchovies for sardines.

APPLE AND CUCUMBER SALAD. (Salade de Pommes et Concombres.)

Procure 1 large cucumber, equal quantity of sliced apples, lemon-juice, salt and pepper, and a little whipped cream or milk.

Season the apples and cucumber with salt and pepper, and sprinkle with lemon-juice. Stir in a little whipped cream or milk, and serve piled in a salad-bowl.

This should be sufficient for 5 or 6 persons.

ARTICHOKE SALAD. (Salade d'Artichauts.)

Have ready some cooked globe artichokes and Vinaigrette sauce (p. 124).

Let the artichokes become quite cold, then serve in a salad-bowl or dish, and hand the sauce separately.

Allow 1 small artichoke or ½ a large one to each person.

ASPARAGUS SALAD. (Salade d'Asperges.)

Have ready 50 heads of cooked asparagus and some Mayonnaise, Vinaigrette, or some Salad sauce (pp. 123 and 124).

Let the asparagus remain on ice for 2 or 3 hours, then coat the tips with sauce, dish up neatly and serve.

This should be sufficient for 5 or 6 persons.

BANANA SALAD. (Salade de Bananes.)

To 6 medium-sized bananas allow 1 gill of Mayonnaise sauce (p. 122), a few sprigs of watercress, and a little finely-chopped parsley, olive oil, lemon-juice, and salt.

Peel the bananas and cut them into rounds ⅛ of an inch thick, and pile them up in a glass dish. Place some watercress round the bottom, and sprinkle it with equal parts of lemon-juice and olive oil, and a little salt. Pour the mayonnaise sauce over the bananas, and sprinkle the parsley on the top.

This should be sufficient for 6 or 7 persons.

BEETROOT AND ONION SALAD. (*See* Onion Salad, p. 114.)

Use 1 part of thinly-sliced onion and 2 parts of sliced and pickled beetroot.

Allow 1 good spoonful of salad to each person.

BEETROOT SALAD. (Salade de Betterave.)

With 1 or 2 good-sized cooked beetroots have ready some salad dressing, celery or horseradish.

Arrange stamped-out or plain slices of beetroot overlapping each other closely, moisten with Salad dressing (pp. 123–124), and serve garnished with shredded celery, or tufts of scraped horseradish.

This should be sufficient for 4 or 5 persons.

BRUSSELS SPROUTS SALAD. (Salade de Choux de Bruxelles.)

Have ready 2 lb. of cooked Brussels sprouts, a small cooked beetroot, and some Salad dressing (p. 123).

Toss the sprouts lightly in a little salad dressing, pile in a salad-bowl, and decorate with beetroot.

This should be sufficient for 5 or 6 persons.

CAULIFLOWER SALAD. (Salade de Choufleur.)

Prepare and cook 1 medium-sized cauliflower and have ready some Salad dressing (pp. 123–124) and some cress and cooked beetroot for garnish.

When cold, break the cauliflower into sprays, toss these lightly in salad dressing, and serve garnished with cress and beetroot.

This should be sufficient for 4 or 5 persons.

CELERY AND CUCUMBER SALAD. (Salade de Concombre et Céléri.)

With 1 head of celery and 1 cucumber take 2 or 3 bunches of small red radishes, ½ a teaspoonful of finely-chopped gherkin, ½ a teaspoonful of finely-chopped parsley, 2 hard-boiled eggs, some Mayonnaise sauce (p. 122), or Salad dressing (pp. 123–124), salt and pepper.

Use only the white part of the celery; trim and wash it, shred lengthwise into fine strips, let it remain in cold water for about ½ an hour, then drain and dry thoroughly. Peel the cucumber thinly, cut it across into 1½-inch lengths, and shred them in the same way as the celery. Mix the salad dressing, celery, cucumber, and a seasoning of salt and pepper thoroughly together, heap it up in the bowl, surround the base with the radishes, garnish with slices of hard-boiled egg, sprinkle over the gherkin and parsley, and serve.

This should be sufficient for 6 or 7 persons.

CHICKEN SALAD. (Salade de Volaille.)

With 1 boiled chicken take 2 heads of lettuce, 2 strips of white celery, 2 hard-boiled eggs, 12 stoned olives, 1 tablespoonful of capers, 1 tablespoonful of strips of gherkin, 1 gill of Mayonnaise sauce (p. 122), 1 tablespoonful of tarragon vinegar, salt and pepper.

Remove the bones, and cut the flesh into small neat pieces. Wash the lettuce and dry it thoroughly; wash the celery and cut it into dice. Mix the chicken, celery, and lettuce together in a basin, add the vinegar, and season with salt and pepper. Transfer to a salad-bowl, pile high in the centre, cover with mayonnaise sauce, garnish with alternate groups of lettuce leaves, quarters of hard-boiled egg, stoned olives, shredded gherkin and capers, and serve.

This should be sufficient for 6 or 7 persons.

COLD MEAT SALAD À LA FRANÇAISE. (Salade de Viande à la Française.)

Take 1½ lb. of cold roast or boiled meat, 4 anchovy fillets, 2 shallots, 2 tablespoonfuls of salad-oil, 1 tablespoonful of wine vinegar, ½ a teaspoonful of finely-chopped parsley, 1 teaspoonful of French mustard, salt and pepper. For garnishing: shredded pickled gherkins and finely-chopped capers.

Cut the meat into strips about 2½ inches in length and ½ inch in width. Chop the shallots and fillets of anchovy finely, put them into a basin, add ½ a teaspoonful of parsley, the oil, vinegar and mustard, season with a little salt and

SALADS

pepper, then stir in the slices of meat, cover, and put aside for 2 hours, stirring occasionally. When ready to serve, arrange the salad in a pyramidal form in a salad-bowl, garnish with strips of gherkin and chopped capers, and serve.

This should be sufficient for 6 or 7 persons.

CRAB SALAD. (*See* East Indian Salad, p. 110.)

CRESS SALAD. (Salade au Cresson.)

Procure a good bunch of watercress, half as much mustard and cress, 2 hard-boiled eggs, some French Orleans vinegar, tarragon vinegar, Provence oil, mignonette pepper, and salt.

Mix together equal quantities of French Orleans vinegar, Provence oil, and tarragon vinegar. Season this with salt and mignonette pepper. Have ready some small cress and watercress, thoroughly washed and trimmed. Drain well, and pour over the prepared dressing. Mix well but lightly, and put into a salad-bowl. Garnish with hard-boiled eggs.

This should be sufficient for 5 or 6 persons.

CUCUMBER SALAD. (Salade de Concombre.)

With 1 cucumber take ½ a teaspoonful of finely-chopped parsley, vinegar, salad-oil, salt and pepper.

Peel the cucumber thinly, cut it into very thin slices, and place them in a salad-bowl or dish. Mix 2 parts of salad-oil with 1 part of vinegar, add the parsley, salt and pepper to taste, stir well, and pour over the cucumber.

This should be sufficient for 4 or 5 persons.

CURRY SALAD. (Salade de Homard au Kari.)

Have ready 1 lobster coarsely flaked, 1 cucumber sliced, 1 teaspoonful each of finely-chopped shallot, and mango chutney, 1 teaspoonful of curry-paste, 3 tablespoonfuls of salad-oil, cayenne, shredded lettuce, and endive.

Mix the shallot, chutney, curry-paste, a good pinch of cayenne and the oil well together. Add the lobster and cucumber, and, when well mixed, serve on a bed of lettuce, and garnish with endive.

This should be sufficient for 4 or 5 persons.

DUTCH SALAD. (*See* Flemish Salad, p. 111.)

EAST INDIAN SALAD. (Salade à l'Indienne.)

To 1 large crab allow 1 gill of tarragon vinegar, 1 teaspoonful of chilli vinegar, 1 tablespoonful of salad-oil, 1 anchovy, shredded celery, lettuce, endive, cayenne and salt.

Pound the anchovy and crab in a mortar, add the salad-oil, vinegar and seasoning to taste, and serve garnished with celery, lettuce and endive. Another variety of crab salad is made by mixing the prepared crab with shredded lettuce, endive, celery, etc.

This should be sufficient for 4 or 5 persons.

EGG SALAD. (Salade aux Œufs.)

Take 6 hard-boiled eggs, 1 crisp lettuce, a few slices of beetroot, 1 tablespoonful of capers, $1\frac{1}{2}$ teaspoonfuls of chopped parsley, 1 slice of toasted bread, 2 tablespoonfuls of cream (optional), and 1 tablespoonful of Mayonnaise sauce (p. 122).

Cut the eggs across into rather thick slices; wash, trim, and dry the lettuce thoroughly; if cream is used, whip it stiffly, and add it, with a teaspoonful of parsley, to the mayonnaise sauce. Place the round of toast in a salad-bowl; upon it arrange a layer of lettuce leaves, then a layer of mayonnaise, cover with slices of egg, and season with salt and pepper. Repeat until the materials are used, piling the centre somewhat high, garnish with the capers and slices of beetroot, sprinkle on the remainder of the parsley, and serve.

This should be sufficient for 6 or 7 persons.

ENDIVE SALAD. (Salade de Chicorée.)

Have at hand 2 heads of endive, cress, shredded celery, boiled beetroot, and Salad dressing (pp. 123–124).

Separate the endive into tufts, toss these in salad dressing, pile them high in a salad-bowl, and garnish with cress, celery and beetroot.

This should be sufficient for 4 or 5 persons.

ENGLISH SALAD. (Salade à l'Anglaise.)

Take 2 shredded lettuces, a bunch of watercress, a handful of mustard and cress, a bunch of radishes sliced, a few spring onions finely sliced, sugar, salt, pepper, equal parts of oil and vinegar, and some sliced tomatoes.

Mix together the lettuce, cress, radishes and onions. Add

a little sugar and a seasoning of salt and pepper to the oil and vinegar, pour it over the salad, and serve garnished with sliced tomatoes.

This should be sufficient for 6 or 7 persons.

FISH SALAD. (Salade de Poisson.)

With 1 lb. of cold fish have ready some Mayonnaise sauce (p. 122), or other salad dressing, lettuce, endive, cress, and suitable fish garnish.

Separate the fish into large flakes, place it alternately with layers of lettuce, etc., in a salad-bowl, covering each layer very lightly with mayonnaise or other salad dressing. Decorate with olives, sliced beetroot, prawns, gherkin, or any suitable fish garnish.

This should be sufficient for 5 or 6 persons.

FLEMISH SALAD. (Salade à la Flamande.)

Have ready equal quantities of cooked Brussels sprouts, boiled potatoes sliced, sprays of boiled cauliflower, sliced beetroot, and chopped apples. To 1 bowl of salad allow 1 small herring separated into small flakes and some mayonnaise or other Salad dressing (pp. 123-124).

Mix all the ingredients together, add salad dressing to taste, and serve.

Allow 1 good spoonful of salad to each person.

GAME SALAD. (Salade de Gibier.)

With 1 lb. of the remains of any kind of cold game take 1 hard-boiled egg, 2 lettuces, cayenne, pepper and salt, some Mayonnaise sauce (p. 122) and pickled beetroot for garnish.

Remove the bones, and cut the flesh into dice of medium size. Wash, trim and dry the lettuce, and tear it into shreds. Stamp out some star-shaped pieces of white of egg, chop up the remainder of the egg, and mix it with the meat. Arrange the meat, lettuce, and mayonnaise in alternate layers in a salad-bowl, raising the centre in a pyramidal form, and add a sprinkling of salt and pepper to each layer. Cover the surface with a thin layer of mayonnaise sauce, garnish with stars of sliced beetroot and hard-boiled yolk of egg, and serve.

This should be sufficient for 5 or 6 persons.

GREEN PEA AND BEAN SALAD. (Salade de Petits Pois et Haricots Verts.)

Have ready 1½ lb. of cooked green peas, cooked French beans, 1 small cooked beetroot, 2 hard-boiled eggs, ½ a teaspoonful of finely-chopped parsley, a clove of garlic, and some Salad dressing (p. 123).

For this salad preserved peas and beans may be used. When using fresh ones boil them separately in slightly salted water containing a small piece of soda, drain well, and, when cold, cut the beans into 1-inch lengths. Cut the clove of garlic in two, and rub the inside of the salad-bowl with the cut side. Mix the peas and beans with 2 or 3 saladspoonfuls of dressing, and a seasoning of salt and pepper, garnish with rings of hard-boiled egg and slices of beetroot, sprinkle the parsley over, and serve.

This should be sufficient for 6 or 7 persons.

HORSERADISH SALAD. (Salade de Raifort.)

Take ¼ of a lb. of finely-scraped horseradish, some cress, and Mayonnaise sauce (p. 122).

Moisten the horseradish with mayonnaise, and garnish with cress.

This should be sufficient for 6 or 7 persons.

ITALIAN SALAD. (Salade à l'Italienne.)

Prepare and cook equal parts of carrots, turnips, potatoes, beetroot, Brussels sprouts, French beans, and sprigs of cauliflower. Also some Tartare sauce (p. 124).

Cut the carrots, turnips, potatoes and beetroot into ½-inch slices and mix all well together with the other vegetables, moisten with the sauce, and serve.

Allow 1 good spoonful to each person.

Note.—This salad is frequently prepared in an ordinary basin mould, which is masked with aspic, and afterwards decorated with tomatoes and other vegetables.

JAPANESE SALAD. (Salade à la Japonaise.)

Procure 3 medium-sized truffles, 3 medium-sized cold boiled potatoes, 18 cooked mussels, 1 teaspoonful of blanched onion finely-chopped, 1 teaspoonful of finely-chopped parsley, 12 small fillets of anchovy, small lettuce leaves, ½ a wineglassful of champagne (optional), nutmeg, salt and pepper.

EGG DISHES

1. Eggs à la Courtet. 2. Eggs à la Dreux. 3. Anchovy Eggs.

SALADS

Chop the truffles coarsely and mix with the potatoes previously cut into dice, add a pinch of nutmeg, and a seasoning of salt and pepper together, and the champagne (if used). Let it stand for 2 hours, then add the mussels, onion and parsley, and serve garnished with lettuce leaves and fillets of anchovy.

This should be sufficient for 6 or 7 persons.

LENTIL SALAD. (Salade de Lentilles.)

With 1 pint of cooked lentils take ¼ of a pint of shredded celery, 1 tablespoonful of finely-chopped cooked onion, and some Salad dressing (p. 123).

Place a little salad dressing in a salad-bowl, put in the lentils, etc., mix well, and garnish with beetroot, cress, or radishes.

This should be sufficient for 6 or 7 persons.

LETTUCE SALAD. (Salade de Laitue.)

Take 2 heads of cabbage lettuce, 2 hard-boiled eggs, 3 salad-spoonfuls of salad-oil, 1 saladspoonful of tarragon vinegar, ½ a teaspoonful of chopped parsley, salt and pepper.

Trim, wash and dry the lettuce thoroughly, tear it into shreds, and place it in a salad-bowl. Put about 2 saltspoonfuls of salt and ½ a saltspoonful of pepper into the saladspoon, fill it with tarragon vinegar, stir until the salt is dissolved, then pour the contents of the spoon over the salad. Add the 3 saladspoonfuls of salad-oil, mix the salad thoroughly, place on the top the eggs cut into quarters, sprinkle over the chopped parsley, and serve.

This should be sufficient for 5 or 6 persons.

LOBSTER SALAD. (*See* Recipe, p. 48.)

MIXED VEGETABLE SALAD. (Salade de Légumes à la Jardinière.)

Have ready 1 small cooked cauliflower, 1 small cooked beetroot, 1 small cucumber, 2 or 3 firmly-cooked potatoes, 2 firm tomatoes, 1 crisp lettuce, and ⅓ of a pint of Mayonnaise sauce (p. 122), or Salad dressing (p. 123).

Divide the cauliflower into small sprays, cut the beetroot and potatoes into fine strips, slice the cucumber and tomatoes. Place all these ingredients in layers in a salad-bowl, piling somewhat high in the centre, and season each layer with salt and pepper. Pour over the salad dressing, and garnish with a border of lettuce, previously well washed and dried.

This should be sufficient for 6 or 7 persons.

MUSHROOM SALAD. (Salade aux Champignons.)

With ½ a pint of preserved mushrooms (champignons) sliced, take 2 tablespoonfuls of shredded celery, 1 tablespoonful of shredded truffle, lettuce, hard-boiled eggs, sliced beetroot, and some Mayonnaise sauce (p. 122).

Mix together the mushrooms, celery and truffles, stir in a little mayonnaise, and pile the mixture on a bed of lettuce. Garnish with sections of egg and slices of beetroot.

This should be sufficient for 4 or 5 persons.

ONION SALAD. (Salade d'Oignons.)

Have ready 1 lb. of large mild onions, some finely-chopped parsley, pepper and salt, oil and vinegar.

Peel the onions, cover them with cold water, bring to boiling-point, and drain. Let them remain in cold water for 6 or 7 hours, changing the water repeatedly. Slice thinly, season with salt and pepper, moisten slightly with vinegar, and more liberally with oil, sprinkle lightly with parsley, then serve.

This should be sufficient for 5 or 6 persons.

OYSTER AND CELERY SALAD. (Salade de Huîtres.)

To 24 oysters allow 1 head of celery parboiled and shredded, ½ a small white cabbage parboiled and shredded, some Mayonnaise sauce (p. 122), oil and vinegar.

Blanch the oysters, and let them remain in the water until they lose their flabbiness. When quite cold, mix the celery and cabbage together, moisten slightly with oil and vinegar, and turn the mixture into a salad-bowl. Place the oysters on the top, coat lightly with mayonnaise, and serve.

This should be sufficient for 6 or 7 persons.

POTATO SALAD. (Salade de Pommes de Terre.)

Take 1½ lb. of small potatoes, ¼ of a lb. of lean bacon, 1 very small onion finely chopped, 1 teaspoonful of finely-chopped parsley, 1 tablespoonful of Mayonnaise sauce (p. 122), vinegar, salt and pepper.

Boil the potatoes in their skins, peel, and slice them whilst hot. Cut the bacon into dice, fry it until nicely browned, then drain well from fat, and put it into a basin with the sliced potato and onion. Season with salt and pepper, stir in the mayonnaise sauce, and about 2 tablespoonfuls of vinegar. Mix carefully so as not to break the potato, and serve in a salad-bowl with the surface sprinkled with the finely-chopped parsley.

This should be sufficient for 6 or 7 persons.

RED CABBAGE SALAD. (Salade au Chou rouge.)

Procure a small red cabbage, 1 pint of malt vinegar, 2 tablespoonfuls of salad-oil, 1 tablespoonful of salt, and 1 salt-spoonful of cayenne pepper.

Shred the cabbage finely and mix the ingredients well together, let the salad stand for 2 days, then use.

This should be sufficient for 6 or more persons.

ROMAN SALAD. (Salade Romaine.)

Have ready 2 cos lettuces, 1 finely-chopped onion, a little honey, and vinegar.

Thoroughly wash, trim, and dry the lettuce, separate it into small pieces, season it with vinegar sweetened to taste with very little honey, and sprinkle over with onion.

This should be sufficient for 4 or 5 persons.

RUSSIAN SALAD. (Salade Russe, au maigre.)

Prepare 1½ pints of Mayonnaise sauce (p. 122), and have ready 1 small cauliflower, 1 gill of cooked green peas, 1 gill of mixed vegetables (dice of carrot, turnip, and French beans), 3 new potatoes, 2 tomatoes, 2 gherkins, 1 truffle, salt and pepper. For garnishing : shredded smoked salmon, ¼-inch dice of hard-boiled white of egg, shredded beetroot, stoned olives, fillets of anchovy, and capers.

Divide the cauliflower into small sprays, boil them and the peas, carrot, turnip and beans separately, and drain well. Boil the potatoes, and when cold cut them into neat strips ; cut the tomatoes into moderately-thin slices, shred the gherkins and truffle finely. When all the cooked ingredients are cold and well drained, arrange them with the tomatoes, gherkins, and truffle in distinct layers in a salad-bowl. Season each layer with a little salt and pepper, and cover lightly with mayonnaise sauce, pile the salad high in the centre, and cover the surface lightly with mayonnaise. Decorate with small groups of shredded salmon, shredded beetroot, dice of white of egg, olives, capers and fillets of anchovy. Serve the remainder of the sauce separately.

This should be sufficient for 6 or more persons.

Note.—This salad is frequently prepared in a cylindrical-shaped mould with suitable border. First mask the mould with aspic, and tastefully decorate with the available vegetables.

SARDINE MAYONNAISE. (Mayonnaise de Sardines.) (*See* Spanish Sardine Salad, p. 117.)

Substitute Mayonnaise sauce (p. 122) for the vinegar.

SHAD'S ROE SALAD. (Salade au Frai d'Alose.)

Procure 3 cooked shad's roes, some shredded lettuce, endive, beetroot, Mayonnaise sauce (p. 122), oil, vinegar, salt and pepper.

Slice the roes thinly, season liberally with salt and pepper, sprinkle with vinegar, and moisten well with oil. Let them remain for 2 hours, then place them on a bed of lettuce, coat lightly with mayonnaise, and decorate with tufts of endive and sliced beetroot.

This should be sufficient for 6 or 7 persons.

SHRIMP SALAD. (Salade d'Écrevisses.)

With 1 pint of picked shrimps take 2 or 3 tablespoonfuls of Mayonnaise sauce (p. 122), sliced cucumber, and shredded lettuce.

Stir the sauce into the shrimps, pile the mixture in a salad-bowl or dish, garnish tastefully, with cucumber and lettuce, then serve.

This should be sufficient for 5 or 6 persons.

SPANISH SALAD. (Salade Espagnole.)

Peel a large Spanish onion, cut it into very thin slices; with this mix a finely-sliced cucumber and 6 firm but ripe tomatoes also cut into slices. Season with salt, pepper, oil and vinegar, and sprinkle some finely-grated Parmesan cheese between each layer. Garnish with stoned Spanish olives, and serve.

This should be sufficient for 5 or 6 persons.

SALADS

SPANISH SARDINE SALAD. (Salade de Sardines à l'Espagnole.)

Take 12 or 14 sardines, 2 tablespoonfuls of capers, 1 crisp lettuce, stoned Spanish olives, Anchovy butter (p. 102), vinegar, salt and pepper.

Remove the skin and bones from the sardines, and divide them into short pieces. Wash and dry the lettuce thoroughly, tear it into fine shreds, put it into a basin with the sardines and capers, season with salt and pepper, add a little vinegar, and mix well together. Arrange the salad in a salad-bowl, piling it high in the centre, garnish with the olives filled with anchovy butter, and serve.

This should be sufficient for 6 or 7 persons.

SPINACH AND EGG SALAD. (Salade d'Épinards aux Œufs.)

Have ready 1 quart of young spinach leaves, 6 spring onions chopped, 3 or 4 hard-boiled eggs, oil, vinegar, and a seasoning of salt and pepper.

Wash the spinach free from grit, dry it thoroughly, and mix with it the onions. Add a few drops of vinegar to 1 tablespoonful of oil, season with salt and pepper, pour it over the spinach, and mix well. Turn into a salad-bowl, garnish with sections of egg, and serve. A salad of cooked spinach may be made by pressing the puree into a mould or moulds, which, when cold, are turned out and garnished with sections of egg.

This should be sufficient for 5 or 6 persons.

SUMMER SALAD. (Salade d'Été.)

To 2 or 3 lettuces shredded allow 2 handfuls of mustard and cress, 12 radishes sliced, ½ a cucumber sliced, and some Salad dressing (p. 123).

Place a little salad dressing at the bottom of a salad-bowl, put in the lettuce, etc., and serve when well mixed.

This should be sufficient for 5 or 6 persons.

SWEDISH SALAD. (Salade à la Suédoise.)

Take 4 oz. each of cold roast beef, some boiled potatoes, firm apples and pickled herring, all cut into dice, 3 anchovies washed, filleted and coarsely chopped, 1 tablespoonful each of chopped gherkin, capers, hard-boiled egg, tarragon and chervil, 24 turned olives, 12 oysters, oil and vinegar.

Mix all but the oysters together, moisten with a little oil and vinegar, and place the oysters on the top.

This should be sufficient for 4 or 5 persons.

SWEETBREAD AND CUCUMBER SALAD. (Salade de Ris-de-Veau et Concombre.)

Have ready a calf's sweetbread cooked and thinly sliced, $\frac{1}{4}$ of a cucumber thinly peeled and sliced, lettuce shredded, and some Salad dressing (pp. 123–124) and Mayonnaise sauce (p. 122).

Toss the lettuce in a little salad dressing, turn it into a salad-bowl, and arrange the sweetbread on the top, cover lightly with mayonnaise, garnish with cucumber, and serve.

This should be sufficient for 3 or 4 persons.

SWISS SALAD. (Salade Suisse.)

With 3 tablespoonfuls of potato take 2 tablespoonfuls of tongue, 2 tablespoonfuls of beetroot, 2 tablespoonfuls of carrot, 1 tablespoonful of apple, all shredded and all cooked except the apple, 1 cooked fresh herring finely flaked, and some Salad dressing (p. 123).

Mix all well together, moisten slightly with salad dressing, and serve piled in a salad-bowl.

This should be sufficient for 4 or 5 persons.

TARTARE SALAD. (Salade à la Tartare.)

Have ready equal quantities of shredded cold meat, celery and cooked potato, some Tartare sauce (p. 124), endive or beetroot, salt and pepper.

Mix the meat, celery and potato together, sprinkle liberally with salt and pepper, and stir in a little tartare sauce. Serve garnished with tufts of endive or sliced beetroot.

Allow 1 good spoonful of salad to each person.

TOMATO SALAD. (Salade de Tomates.)

Take 6 firm medium-sized tomatoes, 1 teaspoonful of finely-chopped parsley, 2 teaspoonfuls of salad-oil, 1 tablespoonful of vinegar, 1 teaspoonful of mixed mustard, and a seasoning of salt and pepper.

Scald the tomatoes in boiling water for 1 minute, drain

SALADS

on a cloth, and carefully remove the stems and skin. When cool, cut them into thin slices, and place them in a salad-bowl. Put 2 saltspoonfuls of salt and 1 saltspoonful of pepper into a basin, add the mustard, pour in the vinegar and oil, and mix thoroughly with a wooden spoon. When ready to serve, add the chopped parsley to the dressing, and pour it over the tomatoes.

This should be sufficient for 5 or 6 persons.

TOMATO AND ARTICHOKE SALAD. (Salade d'Artichauts et Tomates.)

Procure 6 tomatoes, 6 or 8 cooked artichoke bottoms (tinned ones will serve), and make some Mayonnaise sauce (p. 122).

Split the artichoke bottoms in halves, and slice the tomatoes. Arrange neatly in a salad-bowl or dish, pour over a little sauce, and serve.

This should be sufficient for 5 or 6 persons.

TOMATO AND CHIVES SALAD. (*See* Tomato and Onion Salad.)

Substitute 1 dessertspoonful of finely-chopped chives or very young spring onions for the cooked onion.

TOMATO AND ONION SALAD. (Salade aux Tomates.)

Have ready 6 medium-sized tomatoes sliced, 1 large onion, and some Salad dressing (p. 123).

Boil or bake the onion until three-parts cooked. When cold, chop it not too coarsely, sprinkle it over the sliced tomatoes, add a little salad dressing, then serve.

This should be sufficient for 4 or 5 persons.

TRUFFLE SALAD. (Salade aux Truffes.)

Take equal parts of finely-shredded truffles and celery, some Mayonnaise sauce (p. 122), and hard-boiled eggs.

Mix the truffles and celery together, stir in the mayonnaise, and pile in a salad-bowl. Garnish with chopped whites and sieved yolks of hard-boiled eggs, and serve.

Allow a small spoonful to each person.

TURNIP SALAD. (Salade de Navets.)

Have ready some cold boiled turnips, sliced beetroot, Salad dressing (p. 123).

Slice the turnip thickly, cut the slices into strips, and pile them in a salad-bowl. Pour a little salad dressing over them, and garnish with beetroot.

Allow a good spoonful to each person.

WALNUT AND CELERY MAYONNAISE. (Mayonnaise de Céléri et Noix.)

Procure 2 or 3 strips of white celery finely shredded, $\frac{1}{2}$ a pint of peeled walnuts, 2 tablespoonfuls of stiff Mayonnaise sauce (p. 122), 1 tablespoonful of thick cream (optional), salt and pepper. For garnishing : watercress or small red radishes.

Cut the walnuts into small pieces, mix them with prepared celery, season with a little salt and pepper, and add gradually the mayonnaise and cream (if used). Dress in a pile on a vegetable dish or a small flat salad-bowl, garnish with a few sprigs of watercress or small radishes, and serve with roast poultry or game.

This should be sufficient for 4 or 5 persons.

WINTER SALAD. (Salade d'hiver.)

Take 1 small head of celery, $\frac{1}{2}$ a cooked beetroot, 3 or 4 cold potatoes, $\frac{1}{2}$ a teaspoonful of finely-chopped parsley, some Salad dressing (p. 123), salt and pepper.

Peel and slice the beetroot, slice the potatoes, shred the celery, but not too finely. Arrange the prepared vegetables in separate layers, seasoning each layer with a little salt and pepper. Pour over 5 tablespoonfuls of salad dressing, sprinkle on the parsley, and serve.

This should be sufficient for 3 or 4 persons.

CHAPTER VII

SAUCES AND SALAD DRESSINGS

BÉCHAMEL, or FRENCH WHITE SAUCE. (Sauce Béchamel.)

Take $1\frac{1}{2}$ oz. of flour, 2 oz. of butter (or corresponding quantity of white roux), $1\frac{1}{4}$ pints of milk (or white stock), 1 small onion or shallot, 1 small bouquet-garni (parsley, thyme, bay-leaf), 10 peppercorns, $\frac{1}{2}$ a bay-leaf, 1 small blade of mace, and seasoning.

Put the milk on to boil with the onion or shallot, the bouquet-garni, peppercorns, mace, and bay-leaf. Melt the butter, stir in the flour, and cook a little without browning, stir in the hot milk, etc., whisk over the fire until it boils, and let it simmer from 15 to 20 minutes. Strain and pass through a sieve or tammy-cloth, return to the stewpan, season lightly with a pinch of nutmeg, $\frac{1}{2}$ a pinch of cayenne, and $\frac{1}{2}$ a teaspoonful of salt. The sauce is then ready for use.

BROWN SAUCE. (Sauce Brune.)

With $\frac{1}{2}$ a pint of stock or water take 1 oz. of butter or sweet dripping, 1 oz. of flour, 1 small carrot, 1 small onion, salt and pepper.

Cut the carrot and onion into small pieces. Melt the butter in a saucepan, put in the flour and vegetables, and fry until brown. An occasional stir is necessary to prevent the ingredients burning, but if they are constantly stirred they brown less quickly. Add the water or stock, stir until it boils, simmer for 10 minutes, then season to taste, and use. A few drops of browning may be added when the sauce is too light.

CLARET DRESSING.

To $\frac{1}{4}$ of a pint of claret allow 1 teaspoonful of lemon-juice, a clove of garlic, 1 teaspoonful of finely-chopped shallots, and a little salt and sugar.

Mix all the ingredients together, let the preparation stand for 6 hours or longer, then strain, and pour it over a salad previously tossed in a little salad-oil.

MAYONNAISE COOKED. (Mayonnaise cuite.)

Take ½ a pint of milk or single cream, ¼ of a pint of vinegar, 3 yolks of eggs, 1 tablespoonful of salad-oil, 1 tablespoonful sugar, 1 tablespoonful salt, and 1 dessertspoonful mustard.

Mix the oil, sugar, salt and mustard well together in a basin, add the well-beaten yolks of eggs, next the vinegar, and lastly the cream or milk. Stand the basin in a saucepan containing sufficient boiling water to surround it to half its depth, and stir the mixture over the fire until it acquires the consistency of custard. This dressing, if tightly bottled, will keep for several days.

MAYONNAISE, RED. (Mayonnaise rouge.)

Prepare ½ a pint of stiff Mayonnaise sauce (*see* following recipe), and take ¼ pint of tomato purée, salt and pepper.

Mix the ingredients smoothly, and season to taste.

MAYONNAISE SAUCE. (Sauce Mayonnaise.)

Procure 2 yolks of eggs, 1 teaspoonful of French mustard, ½ a teaspoonful of salt, a pinch of pepper, 1 tablespoonful of tarragon vinegar, about 1 pint of best salad oil, and 1 tablespoonful of cream.

Put the yolks into a basin, add the mustard, salt and pepper, stir quickly with a wooden spoon. Add the oil, first drop by drop and afterwards more quickly, and at intervals a few drops of the vinegar. By stirring well, the mixture should become the consistency of very thick cream. Lastly, add the cream, stirring all the while. A little cold water may be added if the sauce is found to be too thick.

In hot weather, the basin in which the mayonnaise is made should be placed in a vessel of crushed ice.

RÉMOULADE SAUCE. (Sauce rémoulade.)

Have ready ½ a pint of salad-oil, 2 tablespoonfuls of tarragon vinegar, 1 teaspoonful of made mustard, 1 raw yolk of egg, a few leaves each of tarragon, burnet, chives, and parsley, 1 saltspoonful of salt, ¼ of a saltspoonful of pepper, and ½ a saltspoonful of castor sugar.

SAUCES AND SALAD DRESSINGS

Blanch the herbs for 1 minute in boiling water, then dry them well and chop them finely. Put the yolk of egg into a small basin, add the salt and pepper, stir briskly with a wooden spoon until very thick, then work in the oil, drop by drop at first, and afterwards more quickly. A few drops of vinegar should be added at intervals during the mixing, and when the desired consistency is obtained, the mustard, herbs and sugar may be stirred in and the sauce used.

SALAD DRESSING.

Procure the yolks of 2 hard-boiled eggs, 4 tablespoonfuls of salad-oil, 2 tablespoonfuls of Worcester sauce or mushroom ketchup, 2 tablespoonfuls of vinegar, 1 teaspoonful of made mustard, 1 teaspoonful of salt, and ½ a teaspoonful of pepper.

Rub the yolks of eggs through a fine sieve, mix with them the salt, pepper and mustard. Stir in the salad-oil, add the Worcester sauce and vinegar gradually, and when thoroughly incorporated the dressing is ready for use. The whites of the eggs should be utilized for garnishing the salad. The above will be found an excellent dressing for cold meat salads to be served with cold meat.

SALAD DRESSING. (Another way.)

With the raw yolks of 2 eggs take 2 tablespoonfuls of salad-oil, 2 tablespoonfuls of thick cream or 1 tablespoonful of milk, ½ a teaspoonful of vinegar (preferably tarragon), ½ a teaspoonful of mixed finely-chopped onion, chervil, salt and pepper.

Add the salt and pepper to the raw yolks of eggs, and stir them with a wooden spoon in a small basin until almost as thick as butter; add the oil, drop by drop, stirring briskly meanwhile, put in the cream or milk, tarragon vinegar, chopped chervil, and use.

SALAD DRESSING. (Another way.)

Have ready 2 tablespoonfuls of cream, 1 tablespoonful of vinegar, ½ a teaspoonful of made mustard, 2 hard-boiled eggs, ½ a saltspoonful of salt, and ¼ of a saltspoonful of pepper.

Bruise the yolks of the eggs with a wooden spoon, add to them the mustard, salt and pepper, and the cream gradually. When perfectly smooth add the vinegar, drop by drop, stirring briskly meanwhile. If preferred, oil may be substituted for the cream. The whites of the eggs should be used for garnish.

SALAD DRESSING, CREAM.

Procure 4 tablespoonfuls of cream, 1 tablespoonful of vinegar, ½ a teaspoonful of made mustard, 1 saltspoonful of castor sugar, and ½ a saltspoonful of salt.

Mix the mustard, salt and sugar smoothly together, stir in the cream, add the vinegar, drop by drop, and use as required.

SOUR CREAM DRESSING.

Procure some sour thick cream and a little salt.

Stir the cream until smooth, add salt to taste, and use as required.

TARTARE SAUCE. (Sauce Tartare.)

Prepare ½ a pint of Mayonnaise sauce (p. 122), and take 1 tablespoonful of chopped gherkin or capers and ½ a teaspoonful of very finely-chopped shallot (this may be omitted).

Stir the gherkin and onion lightly into the mayonnaise, and use as required.

TOMATO SAUCE. (Sauce Tomate.)

With 1 lb. of tomatoes take 2 shallots, 1 bay-leaf, 1 sprig of thyme, 10 peppercorns, 1 oz. of butter, a tablespoonful of flour, 2 oz. of lean ham, 1 tablespoonful of vinegar, salt and pepper.

Melt the butter in a stewpan, add the ham cut small, and the shallots chopped. Cook over the fire, but do not brown. Now add the seasoning, herbs, peppercorns, and tomatoes sliced, sprinkle over the flour, stir all together, and boil for about 20 minutes, or until well reduced. Pass the sauce through a tammy-cloth, heat up, season to taste, and serve.

VINAIGRETTE SAUCE. (Sauce Vinaigrette.)

Take 4 tablespoonfuls of salad oil, 2 tablespoonfuls of tarragon vinegar, ½ a teaspoonful each of finely-chopped gherkin, shallot and parsley, salt and pepper.

Mix all well together, and use as required.

WHITE SAUCE. (*See* Béchamel, p. 121.)

INDEX

	PAGE
Adelaide Sandwiches	94
Alexandra Sandwiches	94
Alpine Eggs	79
Anchovies, Fried	6
Rutland Style	6
Anchovy Aigrettes	29
and Egg Fingers	29
and Egg Sandwiches	95
Biscuits, Royal	7
Butter	102
Croûtes à l'Indienne	30
D'Artois	7
Eclairs	30
Eggs	8
Fingers	31
Rissolettes	31
Rolls	8
Salad	106
Tartlets	8
Toast	31
Angels on Horseback	32
Apple and Cucumber Salad	106
Artichoke Salad	106
Asparagus Salad	106
Salad with Shrimps	9
Baked Eggs	79
Eggs à la Coquette	79
Banana Salad	106
Bâteaux à l'Epicurienne	9
Béchamel Sauce	121
Beef Sandwiches	95
Beetroot and Onion Salad	107
Cassolettes	9
Dressed	10
Salad	107
Bloater Sandwiches	95
Toast	32
Brown Sauce	121
Brussels Sprouts Salad	107
Buttered Eggs à l'Indienne	80
Butter as Hors d'Œuvre	5
Savoury	102
Canapés	10
Cauliflower Salad	107
Caviare and Prawns	11

	PAGE
Caviare Bouchées	32
Croustades	11
Pancakes	32
Patties	33
Sandwiches	96
Cayenne Cheese Fingers	71
Celery à la Greque	11
à la Rivaz	12
and Cucumber Salad	107
Cheese Aigrettes	33
Balls	34
Biscuits	34, 71
Biscuits with Cream	12
Cream, Cold	12
Cream Croûtes	13
Croustades	72
D'Artois	72
Fondue	73
Fritters	73
Méringues	74
Omelet	74
Patties	74
Pudding	75
Ramakins	75
Rings	75
Sandwiches	75, 96
Savouries	71
Soufflé	76
Straws	76, 77
Tartlets	77
Toasted	78
Zéphires	13
Chicken Mayonnaise Sandwiches	96
Salad	108
Sandwiches	96
Chickens' Livers Devilled	35
Claret Dressing	121
Cod's Liver Minced and Baked	35
Liver Quenelles	35
Roe	36
Roe Croquettes	36
Roe Croûtes	37
Roe, Fried	37
Roe Sandwiches	97
Cold Meat Salad à la Française	108
Crab Devilled	37

INDEX

	PAGE
Crab, Dressed	38
Salad	109
Scalloped	38
Crayfish as Hors d'Œuvre	13
Creamed Butter	102
Cress Salad	109
Cucumber as Hors d'Œuvre	14
Barquettes	14
Salad	109
Salad à l'Espagnole	14
Sandwiches	97
Stuffed à la Josephine	14
Curled Butter	102
Curried Eggs	80
Curry Butter	103
Salad	109
Dutch Salad	109
East Indian Salad	110
Egg and Gherkin Sandwiches	97
Croquettes	80
Fritters à la Milanaise	81
Fritters à la Royale	81
Kromeskis	82
Mayonnaise	15
Rémoulade	16
Salad	110
Sandwiches	98
Eggs à la Courtet	82
à la Dijon	16
à la Dreux	82
à la Olivia	16
à la Maître d'Hôtel	83
à la Mornay	83
à la Piémontaise	83
à la Polonaise	84
Alpine	79
Anchovy	8
Baked	79
Baked à la Coquette	79
Buttered à l'Indienne	80
Colbert Style	84
Curried	80
Fricassée of	87
in Aspic	84
in Baked Potatoes	85
in Cases	85
in Gravy	85
Overturned	88
Parmentier	88
Plovers	88, 89
Poached	89, 90
Savoury	91
Scotch	91
Scrambled	91, 92
Scrambled with Anchovies	39
Stuffed à la Russe	17
Stuffed with Prawns	39

	PAGE
Eggs sur le Plat	86
with Black Butter	86
with Ham	86
with Mushrooms	87
with Parmesan	87
with Tongue	87
with White Sauce	87
Endive Salad	110
English Salad	110
Fairy or Feathery Butter	103
Fish Salad	111
Flemish Salad	111
Foie-Gras as Hors d'Œuvre	17
Croûtes	17
Darioles	17
Fleurettes	18
Medallions	40
Sandwiches	98
Sandwiches, Imitation	98
Toast	40
Fricassée of Eggs	87
Game Salad	111
Golden Buck	40
Grape Fruit as Hors d'Œuvre	18
Green Butter	103
Green Pea and Bean Salad	112
Ham and Rice Croquettes	41
Butter	103
Croûtes	41
Ramakins	41
Herring Fillets à la Dubois	19
Roe Croûtes	42
Roe Tit-bits	42
Roes Baked	42
Rolls	19
Horseradish Salad	112
Indian Pineapple Salad	19
Irish Rabbit or Rarebit	43
Italian Salad	112
Japanese Salad	112
Kidney Toast	43
Toast à la Madras	44
Kidneys and Oysters	44
Grilled	44
Lax à l'Huile with Cucumber	20
Lentil Salad	113
Lettuce Salad	113
Lobster Baked	45
Butter	103
Coquilles	45
Creamed	46
Croquettes	46

INDEX

	PAGE
Lobster Cutlets	46
Devilled	47
Devilled sur Croûtes	47
Rissoles	48
Salad	48
Scalloped	49
Macaroni and Cheese	78
au Gratin	49
Cheese	78
Maître d'Hôtel Butter	104
Marrow Toast	49
with Maître d'Hôtel Sauce	50
Mayonnaise Cooked	122
Red	122
Sauce	122
Meat Toast Savoury	50
Melon as Hors d'Œuvre	20
Cantaloup au Marasquin	20
Mince Croustades Savoury	50
Mixed Vegetable Salad	113
Montpelier Butter	104
Moulded Butter	104
Mushroom Salad	114
Soufflé	52
Mushrooms au Gratin	51
Grilled	51
on Toast	51
Stuffed	52
Mustard Butter	104
Olive Sandwiches	21
Olives as Hors d'Œuvre	21
à la Madras	21
à la Tartare	21
in Jelly	22
on Croûtes	22
Omelet Plain	53
with Herbs	53
Onion Salad	114
Overturned Eggs	88
Ox Eyes	88
Oyster and Celery Salad	114
Fritters	53, 54
Sandwiches	99
Sausages	54
Tit-bits	56
Oysters as Hors d'Œuvre	22
Fried	54
in Cases	55
in Shells	55
Jellied	23
on Toast	55
Scalloped	56
with Caviare	23
Parmentier Eggs	88
Plovers' Eggs	23, 88
Eggs in Aspic	89

	PAGE
Plovers' Eggs on Croûtes	89
Poached Eggs	89
Eggs with Ham	90
Eggs with Spinach	90
Eggs with Tomato Sauce	90
Potato Salad	114
Prawns and Shrimps	24
Croûtes à la Tartare	23
in Savoury Jelly	24
Princess Sandwiches	99
Radishes as Hors d'Œuvre	24
Red Cabbage Salad	115
Rémoulade of Artichoke Bottoms	25
Sauce	122
Roes on Toast	56
Rolled Sandwiches	99
Roman Salad	112
Russian Croûtes	25
Salad	115
St. James's Sandwiches	101
Salad Dressings	123
Dressing Cream	124
Sandwiches	100
Salads	105
Salmon Darioles à la Moscovienne	57
Sandwiches	100
Smoked Devilled	57
Sandwiches	93
Sardine and Tomato Sandwiches	100
Butter Sandwiches	100
Canapés	57
Croustades	58
Eclairs	58
Eggs	25
Mayonnaise	116
Patties	58
Toast	59
Sardines Devilled	59
Fried	59
Grilled	60
in Aspic	26
Smoked	26
with Capers	60
with Maître d'Hôtel Sauce	60
with Parmesan	60
with Tomatoes	61
Savoury Butter	102
Eggs	91
Scallops and Mushrooms	61
Fried	62
in Shells	62
Scalloped	62
Stewed	63

INDEX

	PAGE
Scotch Eggs	91
Woodcock	63
Scrambled Eggs	91
Eggs and Ham	91
Eggs with Anchovies	92
Eggs with Mushrooms	92
Shad's Roe Salad	116
Shrimp Salad	116
Toast	64
Shrimps as Hors d'Œuvre	26
Curried	64
Smoked Haddock Croustades	64
Haddock Croûtes	65
Haddock Filleted	65
Haddock Soufflé	66
Soused Fish	26
Salmon	27
Sour Cream Dressing	124
Spanish Salad	116
Sardine Salad	117
Spinach and Egg Salad	117
Sportsman's Sandwiches	101
Sprats Fried in Batter	66
Summer Salad	117
Swedish Hors d'Œuvre	27
Salad	117
Sandwiches	101
Sweetbread and Cucumber Salad	118
Moulded with Asparagus	66
Swiss Eggs	57
Salad	118
Tartare Salad	118
Sauce	124

	PAGE
Toasted Cheese	78
Tomato and Artichoke Salad	119
and Chives Salad	119
and Onion Salad	119
Salad	118
Sandwiches	102
Sauce	124
Tomatoes à la Nicoise	27
and Spinach	67
Baked	68
Devilled	68
Scalloped	68
Stuffed	69
Stuffed with Mushrooms	69
with Shrimps	27
Truffle Salad	119
Tunny Fish	28
Fish with Tomatoes	28
Turnip Salad	119
Vinaigrette Sauce	124
Walnut and Celery Mayonnaise	120
Watercress Butter	104
Welsh Rabbit or Rarebit	70
White Sauce	124
Winter Salad	120
Woodcock Toast	70
Yorkshire Rabbit or Rarebit	70
Zephires	28

BORWICK'S

—the Best

BAKING POWDER

in the World.

Refuse all Substitutes.

Insist on having BORWICK'S.

'TRIDENT'
SALMON & SHRIMP
PASTE

'Salmon and Shrimp' is first favourite among Fish Pastes and *Trident* is fast becoming first favourite among Salmon and Shrimps. There's something special about the *Trident* flavour: something that positively makes a poor appetite good and a good, better.

Maconochies make it   *Good Grocers sell it*

Flavouring is a Fine Art

JUST a drop or two of Lea & Perrins' Sauce added at the right moment to your soups and stews and entrées and savouries, brings out all the character of your ingredients and blends them in a new harmony. Only a few drops, remember. You want to emphasise your original flavours, not drown them. So Lea & Perrins is really economical to use in the kitchen. A 1/- bottle will last a very long time, and the 1/9 size more than twice as long. If you want to know the whole art of using this admirable sauce, consult Lea & Perrins' new cookery book which gives you over a hundred excellent recipes and much practical information about running a modern kitchen.

WRITE FOR A FREE COPY 'SUBTLE SEASONING' TO

LEA & PERRINS

62 Midland Road Worcester